THE CHOSEN ONE:

A Touch From Above

Demetrius P. Guyton

PO BOX 956 ALACHUA FLORIDA 32616

Editorial Services Provided by:

The Remnant Publishing House LLC.

CEO V.Postell Jr.,

Editorial Staff:

Belinda Williams

Erica Hill

ISBN: 10: 1484888162

ISBN-13: 978-1484888162

DEDICATION

First, I would like to appreciate the Lord for making all of this possible. He granted me the grace to go through and the mercy to get to where I am today. I could never ever reimburse you for all You have done, but surely, I can offer my life to You as a living sacrifice. Thanks Father! I love You so much.

Secondly, I must send dedications to my grandmother, Mrs. Ruthie Mae Dunlap. This book is my token of love to you. You have been such an endless blessing to me. I thank the Lord for you. You have been there when others vanished. For that reason, I adore you abundantly. I Love You!

To my biological mother; Ms. Guyton. Thank you so much for being my birth canal. You did what no one else in this world could ever do and that was pushing me into this world through "YOUR" womb. I Love You!

To my biological father, Mr. Gary Burton. Although it was quite disappointing that you and I did not have the bond that we should have had, I have allowed this portion of my life to be a motivating factor to push me into recognizing my full self-worth.

To my hometown; Jasper, Alabama, The Walker Regional Medical Center, the investigators, district attorney, judge, and all of the divine ponds that played their role in this divine development of a seemingly dramatic but deeply preordained sovereign act of God. Thank you so much. You are greatly appreciated. Blessings be upon you.

To my spiritual fathers; Pastor Michael A. Barton, Pastor of Greater Worship Ministries, Eutaw/Marion, Alabama, Bishop Theodis O Kimbrough, Pastor of Greater New Beginnings Baptist Church, Hamilton, Alabama and Apostle Bokassa Montgomery; founder of Warriors For Christ Ministries, Anniston, Alabama. Thank you so much for your sacrifices, love, prayers, support, concerns, and time. It's all appreciated. Every successful person needs a successor and I'm so grateful to have been the one who you passed it down to.

To Mrs. Suzanne O'Rear, my 1st and 3rd grade teacher. I thank the Lord for you. You were my angel that descended from the Heavenly Headquarters and I am very grateful to have such an individual such as you in my life.

I'm so delighted to recognize Mrs. Deossie Williams and the Williams family who has been my diamond in the rough. You're what i call "family" you all took me in as your own child, consoled me, held my hand, and walked me through "it" like a nurturing and loving family does best. Your favorite words to me were, "it's going to be alright". I thank the Lord for you all dearly. Now a word to you, "it's alright now." I love you all.

To Mrs. Jackie Harrell, I admire you as a person and I love you as a "mother". You appeared in my life when I needed you most. I grovel at your feet with love. Thanks for your all.

To Ms. LaJoycelyn Davis and family, Ms. Monica Floyd, Ms. Tiffany Holley, Ms. Tweila Jordan, Lametrius Lewis, and Taneshia Braggs, my "sisters" I'm so grateful to have been in the loving arms in which you all possess. In this process that I had to travel to propel into the presence of God, you were the occasional splashes of fresh water that God used to keep me from becoming too rigid. If I could choose an instrument to describe your love to me, I'd choose a violin, because you all held me so close to your hearts and stroked me with strings of security and happiness. I love you all.

To Mrs. Valerie Watkins, I greatly appreciate you so much for your all. Your prayers, love, thoughtfulness, concerns, support, etc., did not go unnoticed or unappreciated. You are my angel that watches over me all day and night. Your eagle's eye is greatly appreciated. May God continue to so richly bless you that it makes your haters mad as hell. You are a very blessed and highly favored woman of God. Keep that smile. It speaks for itself. I love you.

To Mrs. Brenda Goree, this list of appreciations will be in vain if I don't tell the world that you are "my mama". I tip my hat off to you for being so patient with me. "Phew!!!" What an amazing God we serve (L.O..L.) He heard your prayers. You were the hinge that I could swing on to define the word "understanding". When I was disconnected to the realities of life, you'd give me the wise counsel that ushered a connection to reality. You were very much of a confidant in my life and very fulfilling to my book. I thank the lord for you so much. I love you.

To my lovely "mother" Mrs. Marilyn Gibson, I greet you with sincere love and gratitude. You were very, very sacrificial when it came to your "son". When I called, no matter what it was, your love was extremely and unbelievably unconditional. You always had impressing support for me. You believed in me so much even when I didn't believe in myself. Thank you so much for your endless love. We need more mothers like you. I know god has placed countless stars on your crown, especially for putting up with me. (L.O. L.) I love you.

To Chief Coleman and Sergeant Beck of the Eutaw police department, I know that God is smiling upon you guys for serving with a sincere heart of justice in the time of my bereavement. You guys decided to please God and not the people. You were the Pontius Pilates that washed your hands and said, "I find no fault in him" even when the entire city shouted, "crucify him." We need more law officials in the world with the spirit of God living in them and that will serve the people with sincerity and not allow their positions to give them the launching pads to be evil towards humanity because they feel like they can. God is not asleep and I'm thankful that you guys recognized that. Thank you so much. Blessings be upon you and the entire Eutaw police department in Eutaw, Alabama.

To Mr. Benny Abrams, my kingdom relative that knitted with the Eutaw chief and sergeant of police to so humbly announce that "I'm innocent of the blood of this just man." Words can't explain my gratitude to you. Thank you so much. Blessings be upon you.

Lastly, to our adversary, (that we're constantly warring against) Satan, I thank you for all the years of low self-esteem, poverty, depression, hurt, pain, derision, humiliation, mental, physical, and verbal abuse. I most commemorate you for being a devotee in my life, especially when you tried so hard to deteriorate and destroy me. It was this that crowned me to officially be "the chosen one". What you didn't know was that there was an almighty one that sprinted to my rescue to deviate your plans. Your intentions became an invention for me to invest into the world that the Lord is "The Great I AM".

Many other people played an important part in my life greatly and encouraged me into making this book a reality. I have been very blessed with so many wonderful people who have had such an impact in my life that trying to name them all will be quite challenging. I am extremely fortunate to have so many great friends that if I tried to list them all, I may leave someone out. So instead, let me thank the Lord for all those special people. You know who you are!

FOREWORD

This is an extraordinary book in which Demetrius Pierre' Guyton has shared a powerful testimony of his dramatic life of growing up remembering how he escaped death as an infant and throughout his young life. He paints a picture of Divine Intervention as the predestinated will of God is miraculously played out in his life. This young man has openly dug into the depths of his past and brought to the reader an incredible glimpse at God's invisible hand. After reading this book, you will be blessed and fortified to run the race that is set before you.

This book was written to reach out and touch the lost, hopeless, and helpless. Those that feel that life is meaningless; this book is for you. Please read this awesome heart-touching book and let God whisper in your ear. I promise you that you will be blessed once you allow this book to minister to your soul.

In Pursuit of Prosperity,

Rev. Dr. Kita S. Moss – Youth Pastor
Pilgrim Rest Missionary Baptist Church
Montgomery, Alabama

Bishop Theodis Kimbrough, Pastor of Greater New Beginning Baptist church, Hamilton, Alabama. Demetrius' Pastor, mentor, and father in the ministry.

"I think Demetrius is a great example of an individual who struggled to turn his life around so that he could be a benefit to society. I think that he'll be a great asset to anyone he's working with and that people's lives will be touched and changed."

Dr. Robert Harold Jackson, founder and executive director of (R.A.M) Romanian American Missions organization, Central Baptist church, Decatur, Alabama.

"We, the Jackson family and the Central Baptist church family loves Demetrius so much. He is a dear friend and brother of ours. I thank God for placing him into our lives. We're very proud of him and we decree that no weapon formed against him will prosper. In Jesus' name."

Lashandra Denise Guyton, the wife and mother of Demetrius' unborn daughter, Lametrius Denise Guyton.

"Demetrius was my catalyst to Christ and for that alone, I'm so grateful for the gift that he is to me. I love you Demetrius with all of my heart…"

INTRODUCTION

My name is Evangelist Demetrius P. Guyton. I am a piece of clay who adores The Potter greatly. Indeed, I must state that it is a blessing to be able to reach down into the depths of my soul and communicate with you. It also serves a genuine purpose for me to be able to submit this book to you with sincerity. My life has been a written epistle that can be inserted into the "Holy Bible". I was commissioned by the Holy Spirit to write this book so that souls could be blessed and encouraged. I went through the storms of life and the Lord's mighty hand brought me out for such a time as this. Whatever you may be going through is meaningful. Stay strong and you will become the vessel the Lord will be pleased to utilize for His glory.

It is a pleasure to be able to put my testimony on this recycled paper hoping to recycle someone else's wounded life. Let me tell you, the Lord is real and very powerful. He has brought me through some cramping times. I have seen His incredible and invisible hand at work. I pray that this book reaches into the depth of your soul and resurrects whatever is dead in your life. Your very life is hid in Christ. The very fact that you are alive signifies that the Lord is with you. Yes, through it all, you did not break, deteriorate, or get destroyed. God has a valuable purpose for your life. He loves you and knows that you are very special to God. He cares for you even when you don't care for yourself.

CONTENTS

Demetrius P. Guyton

ACKNOWLEDGMENTS

I'd like to acknowledge everyone that has been overlooked, alienated, walked on walked over, castaway, and left for dead. It's you that's truly God's trophy. If it had not been the Lord that has been on your side… "Where would you be?" My heart is with you all! I been there and I am saying to you If God can do it for me, He can do it for you too!!! Never Let Defeat Have The Last Word!!!

Share With Me My Story…

Chapter 1
The Birth of A Predestined Child

This is the story of my life as told to me by my paternal grandmother mother, Mrs. Ruthie Dunlap. I never knew life could be so good, but I also never thought that life could be this bad. See, there are two sides to every story but in this story I am in search for answers as I journey though the twists and turns of my life from the brink of death as an infant to the realization of my Divine Purpose in God.

On April 28, 1984, somewhere AT 2:25 A.M., I, DEMETRIUS PIERRE' GUYTON was born in Room 2309 at the Walker Regional Medical Center in Jasper, Alabama to Gary Burton and Ms. B. L. Guyton.

According to the details from my grandmother, Mrs. Ruthie Dunlap, I was born a very precious baby. At times, she would boast about my hair and eyes and what an adorable child I was.

Besides, I was her first grandchild.

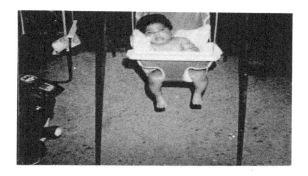

Hospital where I was born & almost died

To my understanding, I had very great parents. People told me how my father was very elated to have had me because I was his first-born child. My father is the oldest child of my grandmother. I was also told that my mother was very compassionate and well known. She was well educated and supposedly, one of the most sincere women you could ever meet. My mother had a child prior to my birth. This was my older brother, Darius Jamarr Henry. We had different fathers but the same mother. He is one year and four

pg. 13

months older than I am. No doubt, I believe that my mother loved her children dearly, but as time passed, the enemy saw an awesome Man of God destroy me. When I was around two months old I suffered experienced a major crisis.

I cannot remember what really went on that day, but from all the information that I have gathered throughout my years of investigation, at the age of two months old, my mother was accused of poisoning me with hydrochloric acid mixed with castor oil along with milk attempting to kill me to cash in on a $25,000 life insurance policy she had taken out on me. The conclusion of this horrific incident was that my facial appearance was disfigured and my nose was collapsed leaving me with no nasal passages. I could not breathe at all through my nose; therefore, I had to learn how to be a mouth breather. Thank God, it did not destroy my will to live. I have heard of numerous reasons why she was accused of doing this to me, but after all the justification, the fact remains that I should have died, but I am still here. After that near death experience, I went through two years of intense surgical attention. Then, at the age of two years old, or slightly over the mark, I was given into the custody of some very, very hateful foster parents. Now, this was a completely frustrating experience. They would make me dress up so uncoordinated. I was never allowed to get my haircut. My only meal would be multiple slices of light bread. At my arrival, I realized that there were three other children there as well. These were my foster parents' two sons and a boy whom I learned later in life was my biological brother. When I got there, my brother was so elated and excited to see me. We grew attached to each other. Yet, being unaware of our kinship, we still called each other "brother" because we were both in the struggle against our hateful foster parents. There were two places I detested to go. You may frown at this, but I truly did hate these occasions. Those occasions were dinner and in society. Those were the most ridiculous moments I have ever encountered. Very embarrassing! My brother and I were dysfunctionally dressed, our hair would be knotty, yet on the flipside, the other two children would be "doing it real big". When my brother and I would go places in society with our foster parents such as grocery stores, gas stations, or to visit others we would be left in the vehicle with the windows rolled up and the doors locked. This was very humiliating for me as a child. We were told that we had better not touch the doors for any reason at all. At dinner, my brother and I would eat slices of light bread and have two glasses of milk to drink. Meanwhile, the others would eat very delightfully.

I recall times when I would whisper to the other boys, "Please can my brother and I have a bite of your food. We're starving!" They would only laugh and say, "No!" and go to the extreme by saying, "Are you crazy! I'm not giving you anything!" Then, they would go tell their parents what I would say to them. Their parents would punish us horribly.

Now, while living with my foster parents, I was still traveling back and forth to my doctor's appointments that were scheduled for me. My grandmother still had authorization to come get me so that I could travel when needed. She would call my foster parents days prior of my appointment to inform them that she will be picking me up on that certain day. For some reason, my foster parents prevented me from phone communications with my grandmother. I could not communicate with my grandmother on the phone for some reason, so my foster parents would say. On the day of my appointed schedule, my grandmother would call to let them know that she was on her way. My foster parents would say, "Demetrius, your grandmother is on her way to pick you up to take you to the doctor, so get ready, but you better not make mention of what's going on in this house." As you know, they were talking about the cruelty they issued me and my brother. Then, they would threaten me of what would happen if said anything about their cruelty. So when my grandmother finally arrived, I'd get into her vehicle acting as if I was the happiest person alive when deeply I was dehydrating for love and care. In my mind, I contemplated deeply and repeatedly to inform grandmother of what was going on, but all I could hear in the back of my skull was what those hateful foster parents would tell me. Nonetheless, I knew that I had to come back to their house. Many times, my grandmother would say, "How's my baby? Is everything o.k.? Are they treating you good?" I'd reply," Mama I am doing great. They're treating me just fine." In all actuality, I was lying to my grandmother. I was in desperate need of assistance. I really did not enjoy being in their company. Those people were crazy. Do not tell them I said it, but they were crazy!

Unknowingly, my grandmother was in court trying to gain custody of me. She would always reiterate her phone number to me "1(205) 387-8307". She would also tell me, "Baby, remember this number just in case you have an urgent matter to discuss with me." While this was going on, my biological mother was incarcerated serving a 20-year sentence for attempted murder. To my understanding, she served at Julia Tutwiler State Prison in Wetumpka, Alabama.

My grandmother and I went to court when I was younger to see if I was able to visit my mother, or have any contact at all. They refused our request and informed me that I should have no contact until I turn twenty-five years old. Therefore, it was a very long time before I heard from my mother.

As far as my foster parents and the household thing went, it got a lot worse. It got to the point where I had to sneak to call my grandmother. While everyone was sleep, I would get my brother to talk to my grandmother about what was going on. She quietly responded, "Don't worry! I'm in the process of possessing Demetrius." My brother hung up the phone and said, "Brother, she said don't worry because she's in the process of possessing you." I was perplexed and mystified at the response, yet I was confident. On April 28TH, 1988, I was awarded into the custody of my grandmother. That was the time of my life. I was finally free from servitude. I felt like an inmate being released from prison after serving a long sentence. Can you imagine that? I recall that day like yesterday or two seconds ago. It was a very great day yet at the same time; it was a very emotional day because I was leaving my brother behind. My grandmother and three detectives came to get me from my foster parent's house.

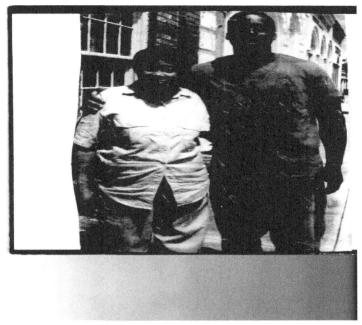

My Grandmother & I

As I was packing my belongings, I saw this look on my brother's face as if the world had fallen on his shoulder. I abruptly stopped packing and approached my brother very emotionally with great tears in my eyes. I heartily informed him to stay strong and know that I love him with my all. Finally, after a few minutes of grief, tears, hugs, and emotional roller coasters, my grandmother stated, "Demetrius, come on it's time to depart." I replied, "Mama, can I bring my brother with me?" She softly answered me, "I'm sorry, but I can't". I nagged at her trying to persuade her to bring my brother along, but it was no use. When I recognized this, I hugged my brother one last huge time, kissed him on his jaw and said, "Don't cry! I love you! If it's meant to be I'll see you again." He answered me with a smile with tears gushing from his eyes.

As I was escorted to the vehicle, my brother assisted me with loading. After loading my property, I turned around and I gave him the deepest stare with tears leaping from my eyes as if two lovers were detaching. In short, I got in the back seat of the detective's vehicle. As we drove off, I turned around waving at my brother goodbye as he was doing the same until we got out of sight.   Finally, I turned back around in the seat and asked my grandmother, "Where are we going?" She said, "Baby we're headed home, I got you all to myself now."

Demetrius and his brother

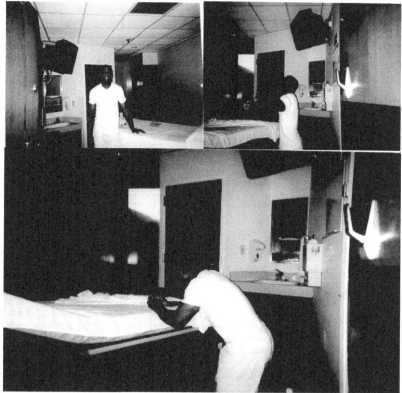

Praising God in the Hospital Room where my Mom attempted to poison me.

Chapter 2
Dissecting My Childhood

I was very elated to be in the custody of my grandmother, but I had to adjust to my new environment very quickly. There was no desire to allow the atmosphere I was accustomed to be abreast to my transition. Everywhere my grandmother would go, I would demand to follow her. My grandmother's household was huge. It was comprised of my grandmother, her husband and her six children, my father, my five uncles and I. My family embraced me and injected so much love inside of me it was unreal. It took a while for me to adjust to the love I received because I was actually unaccustomed to being loved this way.

Not long after my arrival, my father met a lady and relocated from Jasper, Alabama to San Jose, California, where he found himself in a deep dilemma that led him to prison at San Quentin Maximum Security Penitentiary. At this time, I was motherless and fatherless, but my grandmother and uncles assisted me in healing those emotional and mental scars.

There was a gap of months before I would be enrolled in school. In the summertime, I would be allowed to go up to the gym to play but only with adult supervision. I was also allowed to spend nights at other family member's home. One day I was at the gym, and I met an individual who later became my best friend. His name was Acey Cherry Jr. He was a year older than I was. He and his family accepted me for who I was. They embraced me and loved me as their own. Acey and I grew up together from Fruit of the Loom underwear to Hanes boxers. Our friendship was so enveloped that nothing could come between it. As time traveled, I was introduced to others in the area. Most of them remembered who I was because they were familiar with my horrific experience in 1984. It was a huge thing in the eyes of the media for a long time.

Acey was already enrolled in school. He was in kindergarten. Every day when he got out of school, he would come to my grandmother's house to hang out with me.

Before entering school, I underwent a skin-graph surgery. They took skin from around the edges of my ears, my stomach, and the right side of my hip to cover-up the major scars on my face. They also tried to perform plastic surgery on my nose so I could have some nasal passages, but it failed. This left me still without nostrils and yet a mouth breather. The Lord's protection and awesomeness allowed me to be able to maneuver and act like the next normal man, if not better.

Shortly afterwards, it was time for me to enroll in school at T.R. Simmons Elementary. I was anxious and nervous at the same time because I was encountering the unknown. I was focused and concentrated on how the people would take me more than anything. It was a palm sweating, heart-racing thing because I was actually leaving my grandmother's house to get on a school bus packed with all kinds of personalities from all over Jasper. The neighborhood I was raised up in was called Frisco. In Frisco, you had to get it how you knew best. It was a place where you learned survival quickly. Jasper, Alabama was a hard-knock city and very rough

My family had to force me to get on the school bus because I was intimidated by the overwhelming curious stares from people. For days, I would not get on the school bus because I was engulfed with so much low esteem. My uncles would drop me off at school on their way to work and they would tell me, "Demetrius, you've got to get on that bus! No one is going to mess with you!" After deep thought, I grew bold and got on the school bus. It was not as bad as I thought it would be; in fact, my best friend Acey was the first individual I saw as I timidly tiptoed on the bus. He stuck out like a sore thumb. I got on the seat with him and we happily road to school. My fear of the other people's curiosity had decreased, even though I knew and felt on the inside that whispers and questions were parading around the bus about my facial appearance. The ultimate question that jogged through my mind was, "What do I say when people ask me what happened to my face? How am I supposed to answer?" Therefore, I give the "paparazzi" a false answer when they would approach me with curiosity. I would tell them I was in a car wreck or I was caught up in a house fire because I was too embarrassed to say that my mother was accused of trying to kill me. As time passed, while I was in Kindergarten, the curiosity of the people intensified. Curiosity about my story had spread all over the whole school, town, county, and community. Low self-esteem was so engraved in me that school was not a desire. Furthermore, instead of going to school, I would go elsewhere to dodge the people's curiosity.

First day in Shriners School & 1st day with Grandma

City where I grew up

Chapter 3
Dealing With My Eternal Man

Dealing with my external man was a very difficult thing to do, because for a long time I couldn't understand that I was fearfully and wonderfully made *(Psalms 139:14)*. The book states that this is the Lord's doing and it's marvelous in our eyes *(Psalms 118:23)*.Nevertheless, I couldn't see how in the world I could be marvelous in God's eyes when I didn't appear to be anything in my own eyes. At least, that is what low self-esteem whispered to me. It got so bad that I stayed out-of-school for at least a month and a half. I would get on the bus and act as if I was really going to school, but in all actuality, I would disappear to an isolated area that I discovered in a wooded area under a pine tree.

Yes, I know this sounds weird, but this was my way of stealing away from the crowd only to cry out to God asking him, "Why? Why me Lord? I didn't ask to be here, so why didn't you allow me to die at first?" I am very persuaded that we have all been in that phase of life before. If you not, then keep on living. To those that have experienced that episode, you can somewhat feel me right?

My kindergarten teacher would call my grandmother in concern of my absence and say, "Why has Demetrius been absent for so many days? Is he o.k.?" My grandmother would reply, "Demetrius never misses any days from school. As a matter of fact, I personally make sure that he's on the school bus every day." This was so true. She did do this for me, but she unaware that I was dodging people's curiosity. At the end of the school hours, I would camouflage in with the crowd, get on the school bus and act as if I had been in school all day.

The pine tree where I would go to was approximately a football field away from the school. Therefore, I could be hid from the public but still have the school under my surveillance. I was relentless with my routine until one day I was caught tiptoeing. When I would go home from school, my grandmother would be on the front porch with this intimidating countenance. I knew something would be wrong, but if she remained quiet, I did also. Finally, my grandmother decided to question my absence. One day, I got off the bus and went into the house with full enthusiasm as if I was actually excited about school only to notice my grandmother sitting on her couch with tears streaming down her eyes. I asked her, "What's wrong?" She gently replied, "Demetrius, where have you been?" I replied, "Mama, what are you talking about? Didn't you see me get off of the bus?" She said, "Baby, your teacher called me informing me that you've been absent from her class for quite a while. What's up with that?" Of course, I lied, telling her false stories, but eventually all of my lies found me. My grandmother was very angry with me for lying to her but she could not feel the penetration of my pain. She never knew what I was wrestling with on the inside and in public. I was like a helium balloon blown up to the maximum and ready to burst at any time. Therefore, I had to go and release my "air" somewhere.

I would be very confidential with my grandmother for a long time about what had me in a headlock. She would tell my uncles to counsel me also, but I was deaf and mute to them as well. One day I was headed to school to do my normal strategy, but little did I know, my grandmother and uncles had placed total and complete surveillance on me. When I arrived at the school, I got off the bus and shuffled to my solitary area. After I got comfortable, suddenly, I heard a voice coming from behind the bushes screaming, "Boy get up off that ground and get in this car now!" I looked to notice that voice was my uncle. Instantly, I gave him a run for his money. I got up and ran swiftly through the bushes. I was familiar with the area so for a while, I camouflaged from my uncle. Seconds of nervousness and deep thoughts passed by and my mind was racing with thoughts of what could happen once I surrendered. I also knew that I had to go back home or live in the woods.

I surrendered and got into my uncle's vehicle. While we rode down the road to my grandmother's house, he asked me personal questions, but I remained silent. When we arrived to my grandmother's house, I thought life was split in half for me. I didn't know what to do or say. Finally, I gave in and expounded on how low self-esteem had me tangled in a spider web of insecurities and uncertainties. After the family's intense discussion and advice, they all agreed to escort me to school making sure that I was in class. We also had a long talk with the principal and the conclusion was to allow me to have schooling in the most comfortable environment available. So, my classes would be after hours with my grandmother and my kindergarten teacher available. Unbelievably, I was promoted from Kindergarten to the first grade.

My first grade teacher was an angel in disguise. Her name was Mrs. Suzanne O'Rear. This lady was sent to me directly from the Heaven Headquarters. She was so wonderful with a heart bigger than the world. One particular day after about four months of being in her class, she brought it to my attention that she wanted to dialogue with me after school. I consented and stayed but we informed my family of what was going on. Her curiosity was extreme about my facial appearance. She also placed her hands of support in my life bountifully. Mrs. O'Rear assisted in me having plastic surgical attention at U.A.B. hospital in Birmingham, Alabama. My family agreed to link up with her and they planned a day to travel from Jasper, Alabama to Birmingham, Alabama.

After entering the hospital, going through the procedures, and being put to sleep, eighteen hours later, I was awaken to recognize that I had my sense of smell. This was my dream come true. I could actually smell. I was the happiest child alive because what was once abnormal to me had become normal. On the entire trip back home, I screamed repeatedly, "I can smell! I can smell!" My grandmother and Mrs. O'Rear seemed to be happier than I was. After the seemingly long journey from Birmingham, Alabama to Jasper, Alabama, I was rolled into my grandmother's house in my wheelchair where a brand new red remote control car awaited me along with other toys. That was my dream toy and I always desired to have a red remote control car.

My family never ceased to appreciate Mrs. O'Rear for what she had done for me. They loved her and opened their hearts tremendously to her. Mrs. O'Rear had become a part of the family. Everyone would brag on how good of a job the surgeons had done, but to me that did not make a hill of beans if I could not see it for myself. Therefore, I repeatedly beseeched them to take me out of the wheelchair so I could see how good I really looked. Finally, they took me into the restroom and allowed me to see what the surgeons had done.

I noticed that I was wrapped up like an ancient mummy. I also noticed that I had rubber tubes in my nostrils to keep my nose open until the swelling and soreness healed. Amazingly, after seeing myself, spontaneously, my body began to ache miserably, especially my facial area. The pain would seemingly increase and intensify. I begin to scream and shout begging someone to please remove those tubes from my nostrils. They wouldn't do it but I could no longer endure the pain and tightness of the swelling on my face. I took strong medication, but it seemed that the very sight of me being stitched and wrapped up brought about mental pain.

I believe with all of my heart that if I were not so anxious to see my appearance, then it would have been all good. Before morning arose, I cried and screamed enough to irritate them to the point of responding to my request. Before they removed my tubes, they informed me one last time, "Demetrius, are you sure that this is what you want us to do? You look very good and it will be greater later."

Due to the seemingly endless pain, I hurriedly shouted, "Yes! Please get these things out of my nostrils." I was much unlearned that this action taken would result to me never having my sense of smell again. The truth is, if you felt the pain I was feeling, I promise that you would have done the same thing. It was a very miserable experience. The next day after removing the rubber tubes from my nostrils, my nasal passages collapsed and it was worse than before. I was informed by Mrs. O'Rear not to worry about coming back to school for a while until I healed completely. In spite of my condition, I excelled in the first grade and was promoted to the second grade.

Chapter 4
From Misfortune To A Miracle

Every kid has a king or a queen on the inside of him or her, but it is up to them to realize that for themselves. The word "motivation" plays a great role in knowing that you possess a greater person on the inside. These days most of the young children have no one to push them to the extreme of who they really could be. Mothers love their children and want the best for them, but they cannot do like a father. In my life, instead of my mother and father being my "motivator", it was my grandmother, Mrs. Ruthie Dunlap. Now, I know that you may be caught with the question, "Why not your uncles? Where were they?" I can agree with your questions because we were in the same household. It looks like they should have been the ones to show me how to be a king, right? Nonetheless, my grandmother was my all.

My uncles were living lives that did not characterize that of a positive role model. In short, I must say that they loved me with their all and if there were any necessities, they' assisted me. They were always there, but they had their own thing going. My grandmother was always there when no one else was. At this time, my eyes of understanding were fully opened, because my inside was screaming, "Where is my motivator?" As time passed, I found out that my father was incarcerated in California. I yearned for a male role model, but there was none around. Even though I was being vice-gripped by my grandmother, I chose willingly to approach the streets, but it was always a huge hole in that optical illusion. My mind could not comprehend it, yet I still desired to possess a male role model.

My 2nd Grade Class

My second grade school year was getting more intense with problems from people and their curiosity. I knew that it was the nature of a curious person to say, "Hey, what happened to your face?" In time, I became quite frustrated with the questions.

My low self-esteem caused my grandmother to unleash total surveillance on me because she knew the direction it led me previously. I went home one day and contemplated on ways to prevent the people from riding me with jokes that had been thrown at me. I knew I had to do something very quickly because if not I would probably lose my mind or have a nervous breakdown.

I endured so much mentally, physically, emotionally, socially and spiritually. Internal tears would leap even when they didn't externally. Well, they came out, but only when I was alone such as in the bathroom and or in the bed under the covers. Really, I would only be partially alone then. So I concluded one night as I was viewing "The Simpsons". I observed how all the people would make jokes at Bart and his appearance. He started to fight them and joke back. So I grasped his concepts and utilized them. I laughed earnestly at the jokes that were being said about me. As a matter-of-fact, I would laugh harder than the actual jokers would. I assumed that this planted a seed in their minds of asking the question secretly, "Hey what's wrong with him? Is he o.k.? I hope he knows that while he's laughing we're talking about him."

Amazingly, that strategy worked for quite a while. After time, that got old to me and I decided to myself, "Forget it! The next one say something stupid at me, I'm swinging." What a wise thing to do! Just fight my way through my daily problems. I did that every day if not every other day. Fighting became my first cousin. The principal had been very acquainted with me. That showed how sincere I was with my decision. My foolish choice led me to a very bad start of my childhood. After my first couple of fights, I grew accustomed to that life. I was not aware that I was digging a deeper ditch for myself.

While in the heat of a battle one day a young lady named Ashley Simon, who later came to be my first girlfriend, called me by name and yelled, "Stop! I mean right now! Demetrius, you're making a complete fool out of yourself!" I looked at her as if she was the fool, but in all actuality, she was true. It astonished me to see Ashley step up in the midst of the crowd and say what she said. She would also get angry at how my peers would downgrade me. Ashley and I got acquainted with each other. She began to pump, prime and pry the king out of me. I also learned that Ashley lived around the corner from where I was living. She would tell me repeatedly, "Demetrius please stop trying to be something that you're not. You are nothing like what you are trying to present to people. Could you please be yourself?" I told Ashley, "How can I be myself when I don't know myself?"

That was an awful feeling because I had to constantly multiply my character in different environments. Ashley replied, "Demetrius, first you have to let those negative friends loose and focus on your education. " I knew this was an angel because it was unprecedented for a second grader to talk with such wisdom. She wanted me to feel good about myself. Eventually, I separated from those peers and grow close with Ashley. Those individuals that would deride me hated me more because I detached from them and attached to Ashley. They would go tell her, "Why do you desire to be his friend? Look at him! He's ugly!" Ashley replied very strongly, "Please, leave my presence and don't return!" Incredibly, she put those fellows on the spotlight. When they saw how sincere she was, they ceased to approach us.

Everyday Ashley's mother, Mrs. Denise Simon, would drop her off at my grandmother's house. We studied and did other normal things friends do together. Acey Cherry Jr. was still involved in my life also. Mrs. Simon would come back at 7:30 or 8:00 p.m. to get Ashley and take her back home. Acey would stay for a long with me. Sometimes, he would spend the night. My grandmother would always pick at me by saying, "Oh! I see, Demetrius, you've found a girlfriend huh?" I would tell my grandmother "No! This is just a good friend and school mate." One particular day, when Ashley came over my grandmother's house to see me, my grandmother asked her, "Do you like my grandson?" Ashley replied, "I do like him as a friend, but I'd love to be his girlfriend". I was like "Whoa!" She really did like me for who I was. My grandmother humorously responded by saying, "Ashley, I guess I'll let you be his girlfriend, but you better treat him right." I love my grandmother even though she can be very silly at times.

Ashley continued to be on my side and with her assistance and pushing me; I passed the second grade and got elevated to the third grade. Now my third grade was shocking and at the same time, it was heaven-positioned because I ended up in Mrs. Suzanne O'Rear's class once again. No, I was not demoted back to the first grade. While I was in the second grade, Mrs. O'Rear had been promoted to be a third grade teacher. Therefore, I was blessed to be in her class again for my third year.

Ashley was right there with me. Acey was there also, but he was in the classroom next door. Mrs. O'Rear was very elated and proud of me. I had a girlfriend, great esteem about myself, and a mind to learn.

Mrs. O'Rear once again encouraged me to have corrective surgery. In short, I informed her that I was not equipped to endure the pain I had to endure previously. If it was going to be anything like before, I did not want it. Mrs. O'Rear agreed to wait until I grew older where I could endure the surgery. Meanwhile, on the other hand, I still had to deal with those haters. Mrs. O'Rears, Ashley, and Acey were yet on my team, disregarding anything negative that approached them about me. Most of the time because of the favor that was on my life, the guys that opposed me would make private plans to hurt me, but when they'd build up the nerves to do so it failed because people would attach to me that I didn't even know. Some of the peers that were associating with me were actually adjoined to them. They would secretly inform me of what was going to occur and I would be privately prepared. What's that! I call it amazing. What about you? If it was not for the Lord on my side when men rose against me... (Psalms 124:1). I believed that many days they would have swallowed me up.

I was still ignorant to the fact that God was shedding His love, protection and tower of safety around me. Ashley loved me because she saw who I was sprouting to be. Apparently, she saw a greater individual inside of me than i saw in myself. Beyond the haters, I enjoyed my third grade year because I was enthusiastic about my education. With the assistance of Ashley and Mrs. O'Rear, I passed the third grade and was promoted to the fourth grade. My grandmother and my uncles were very proud of me and they continued to encourage me to get my education.

My fourth and fifth grade year went completely downhill because the link that connected my chain was broken. It was a hard pill to swallow. Ashley's mother, Mrs. Denise Simon decided to relocate to a town called Cordova, Alabama, which was only about a twenty-minute drive away from my grandmother's house. I could not see her at all anymore but I was still able to converse with her over the phone. I was miserable again because I had to deal with being without Ashley. After a while, I began to fall into the confused, discomforted, and disoriented me again.

Mrs. O'Rear would periodically check on me and Acey would continue to be my motivator in motivating me to blossom in school and in loving myself. By the grace of God, I passed the fourth and fifth grade I was promoted to the sixth grade. Let me tell you, my sixth grade year was a totally different environment, but it was all good because most of the people were with me in elementary school. We were in Maddox Junior High School now and I wasn't a complete stranger at Maddox High. I wasn't as befuddled as I was when I first started kindergarten.

Junior high school was a very attractive atmosphere. As time passed, I played football and basketball. I was involved in many recreations and activities. I had to sneak to play sports and be a part of activities in school, because my grandmother was so protective of me that she didn't want me to get hurt. In spite of her protectiveness, I still engaged in sports and recreational activities. People recognized my skills and began to encourage me to continue to play. I played basketball and I was very good. I also played football later on in high school.

One day as I was walking down the halls going to my next class, I was approached by peers and introduced to gangbanging. From the approach of the peers, I felt a warmth of comfort and love. This seemed to have been the thing that fulfilled my void. I learned through experience that everything that glitters isn't gold. That is a lifestyle that I never want to be inserted into anymore. When I accepted the invitation from my peers to be a part of the Disciple gang, I was asked to be at an orientation that was held at gym where I could go for recreation.

I told my friend Acey that I was asked to be a Disciple. He replied with a scream saying, "No Demetrius! Don't do it!" I also told Ashley over the phone that I was asked to be a disciple and she gave me the exact same response as Acey did. I thought that they were jealous of me being a gang member. So I rebelled at their response and attended the meeting at gym. When I got there, I noticed twenty to twenty five guys awaiting me. Most of them were a lot older than I was. Only about four of my peers that introduced me to this gang life were actually there. As I was attentive to this inauguration, they explained to me that they were my family and that they were there for me. I felt comfortable because they were like big brothers to me. At least I thought they were.

They began to share with me the yeas and nays of the disciple organization. This was what they called receiving knowledge. Wow! What a way to receive knowledge! I think it was crazy. We dialogued for a while. They began to ask me personal questions and I answered them to the best of my ability. Moments later, the head leader of the disciple gang asked me to get down on my right knee. I did as requested. Then the guy pulled out a black and white bandana, folded it up neatly, laid it on the edge of the field where we were, and told me to close my eyes. Being a young wanderer, lost and looking for acceptance, I did all I was asked to do. When I closed my eyes, they said the opening statements of what they called prayer, and began to initiate me in such a brutal way.

They beat me as if I had done something to their child or mother. They kicked me, slapped me, punched, and stomped me senseless. All I could do was protect my face the best way I knew how. As they were beating me, they would holler out, "Grab the flag! Grab the flag! You say you wanted to be a gangster huh?" I couldn't grab the flag because they were demolishing me. Therefore, I took the beating, which seemed forever. Suddenly, a guy arrived in an old beat up burgundy truck. He saw the guys brutalizing me and shouted, "Get off of him! What's wrong with you all? Are you crazy? That's Mrs. Dunlap's grandson! The Dunlap boys will kill you over him! This will lead to some serious trouble once they find this out!" I didn't know who he was, but I thank the Lord for him.

The guys tried to intimidate this individual, but he only got more agitated. He pulled out a pistol on the guys, shot twice in the air, and made them cease from beating me. Afterwards, he hollered, "Demetrius get up and get in the truck!" I could not because I was damaged from the destructive initiation of the disciples. Therefore, when they fled, he helped me to get into his truck. He called my family and informed them of what took place at the gym. My family met us at Walker Regional Medical Center. Yes, this is the exact place I was born. The instant my family saw me, they grew very angry and desired to repay those individuals for what they had done to me. I went into surgery and remained there for quite a while. When I was able to recover from surgery, I was stronger than ever. I made it through, but by me enduring the brutalization, I still considered myself a gangster in heart.

I secretly snuck away and got a tattoo representing who I was and what I had been through. When my grandmother saw my tattoo, she was so upset with me. I gave myself the thug name "G-THANG" and had it tattooed on my right arm. My opportunity to expose to others that I was a thug was very slim, because everywhere I went I was body guarded. One night while everyone was sleep, my mind whispered to me, "Demetrius, this is you opportunity to advertise to the hood that you're not a punk. You're a gangster." So I tip-toed out of my grandmother's house to prove to a people that didn't even care anything about me that I was sincere about who I said I desired to be....A Gangster!

Chapter 5
The Devil Was Messing, But God Was Blessing

From dealing with all the insecurities and uncertainties, I found myself very dedicated and determined to the gangbanging life. With the appearance of things, this optical illusion looked so delighting to possess. So much love would seemingly bloom from the multitudes of my fellow gang members, their walk, their talk was very intriguing, and they stressed unity and love to the extreme. This phrase would always catch my itching ears, "We're going to ride and die together". To me as a kid, I felt a sense of comfort from these words. To someone as lost and insecure as I was, that was a most reassuring thing to hear from my fellow gang members.

The phrase "ride and die together" let me know one thing; that if I had any altercations, the protection was there and I could rely on my "homies". Even though externally it was gratifying to belong to the gang, internally I was completely ripped into a million pieces. I still felt lost and insecure and the questions of "Who am I? Why am I here?" would worry my mind on a daily basis. Those questions would consume my thoughts while tears would leap from my eyes. Around the fellows, I was "superman", but in my aloneness, deep inside I was a lost and confused "Clark Kent" searching for a place of satisfaction and security for my soul.

I didn't know where to start searching. Therefore, at the age of 12, I found myself smoking weed, drinking, and selling large quantities of drugs. This was so astonishing to me, but very heart breaking to my family. They would discipline me repeatedly but it did not matter to me because I had a point to prove. I was so deep into that thug life that the love, concern, support, and advice from family meant nothing to me because the street's love seemed like it was all I ever needed. I started skipping school and hanging out with the fellows on the regular. I would wear my pants below my waist so low, you would have thought that I had used the bathroom on myself and was afraid to let it touch me. I wore black and white bandanas tied around my body in such areas as my head, neck, right arm, back right pocket, and if I had shorts on, I would have a bandana around my right calf.   I thought that I was someone cool, but in all actuality, I was a ruffian that needed refurbishing.

I was so diligent and dedicated to the disciple gang that when the other fellows saw my sincerity they would always send me on life threatening, on the edge missions. These were missions that the other fellows were intimidated to pursue themselves, but I would be the man, or more correctly the fool, who would carry out the mission. Every time the disciples would attempt to do something wrong, they would say, "G-THANG, (they always addressed me as "G-THANG." that was my gang name) we have in mind to do this, and you're the man for this job. This is how we're going to do it and we want you to be the leader." I was captivated by this because it gave me a feeling of respect that they would call me "G-THANG" a name that I created myself. I'd say to myself, "They must really do respect me. They're calling me by a name that I created."   It meant a lot to me as if I was an elite individual with a high title or position.

Soon, I saw that they saw a complete fool in me and that I would do anything to be accepted, even if it meant putting my life on the line. I just wanted to be a gangster. I thought something was so awesome about this life. It was intriguing to my eyes. At times now, as I look back, I slap myself in the head and say, "How could I have ever been so stupid?" I am so glad that Jesus looked past all of that stupidity and saw my need.

It is amazing how the enemy will try to destroy you and abort your youth at the time when you are unlearned at what is really happening. As I got older, slowly but surely, I grew to understand that the enemy's desire was to eliminate the youth. When you are ignorant and unlearned to the facts of life, the enemy will try to greatly deteriorate your purpose.

. Nonetheless, the hand of God was on me through it all. I would go through hell's side door with no consciousness that I was taking a first class trip to hell's eternal damnation and somehow, I would find myself on a streak of gold instead of on a bed of fire. I recall numerous occasions when I would go to do some harm. My intentions would be this, but it would end up being that. God is so awesome. He will be your mind when you don't have one. He will protect you when it's the last thing on your mind. He will think ahead for you.

God was always present in the midst of my bad decisions I made. I never understood why God was being so good to me. Truthfully, we will never figure it out. All we should stand on is the security of knowing that He's God and there's no other like Him. He alone is God! He knows what's best. He also knows how to snatch you out of trouble in the nick of time. You didn't see it then, but eventually you'll see it. That's the benefit of being God's child. It took a long, long time for me to see this because when I was affiliated in the disciple gang, all I desired to do was show my potential. Even during all of my foolishness, people would still approach me and witness to me about the love of Jesus. I'd hear it and respect it greatly, but somehow it went through one ear and out of the other. My strength, joy, and love were in the disciple gang, a group of people that didn't even care anything about me at all.

The more missions I'd fulfill for the gang, the more love I was being shown love and pats I was getting on my back. I can give the disciples some credit because they did stress earnestly to me about education. They'd pull me to the side and tell me to work hard to accomplish my goals and dreams also to get my education. They called it being a "Gangster and a Gentleman". So, I'd continue to go to school, but my motives were wrong. I was just going through the motion and school wasn't desirable to me anymore. I had made a notorious name for myself all over Walker County and other areas. People knew me and heard about me all over. I was well respected in the streets. What else could a young boy ask for? Money, power, and respect, I'd been introduced to all of that.

I'd finally built up enough self-motivation and dignity to walk the streets with my head up high. The gorilla image I portrayed was a shield for my low self-esteem. Needless to say, I was afraid of life and didn't know how to show my cry in any other way. I substituted a lot of my pain with sex, robberies, drug selling, and partying.

My family had gotten so disturbed about me, that they were willing to relocate to another place just to get me from the streets. Eventually, life had gotten so outrageous for me, that it led my grandmother to relocate from Jasper, Alabama to Boligee, Alabama. My grandmother had purchased land in Boligee, Alabama in 1983. It was always a place she could go to relax her mind and let her conscious be free. There was no house there, only land. Finally, she bought an abandoned trailer and had it pulled on her land. It needed major renovation and great work done to it such as painting, replacing floors and windows.

My family patiently waited long enough for me to be promoted in school to the next grade level and before leaving for Boligee. During the summer of 1997, we left for Boligee, Alabama, a place which I knew very little of. I must say that my grandmother loved me so much that she saw me being a better individual in this country town called Boligee, Alabama, which was an unfamiliar area. This relocation was the vehicle to my revolution. I'd repeatedly ask my grandmother, "Why are we moving to this country back wooded place?" She'd reply, "Demetrius, baby you're headed down a road of destruction. Either you're going to get killed or find yourself in so much trouble that it'll take the rest of your life to get clear."

There was nothing greater my grandmother could have done for me. After the hot scorching mid-July day travel from Jasper, Alabama to Boligee, Alabama, we arrived to a trailer, land, horses, cows and trees as far as you could see it. The trailer had no utilities. Therefore, we had to use flashlights to get around. We ate lunches that we prepared before leaving Jasper, Alabama and we slept in sleeping bags. Early the next morning, we arose and went to working on my grandmother's wounded trailer. I mean from dust to dawn we worked on that trailer. We replaced windows in each room, placed new floors down, laid carpet, cleaned out the trailer, well that was my job, because I didn't know how to do the other stuff my uncles and grandfather were doing. We painted the trailer burgundy and green. I saw my grandmother put thousands of dollars in a guy's hand one day for placing a septic tank in her backyard. It amazed me so much, because I did not even know she was "rolling like that". In two and a half months, my grandmother's trailer was completely refurbished, refurnished, and livable. We even had our utilities turned on. I couldn't believe it! We took what appeared to be nothing and made it into something beautiful... A HOME.

At the beginning, I was very perplexed, because of the decision to move to Boligee and the sacrifices that move required me to make was insignificant, but my grandmother knew something and had a dream of a change and we followed suit. The following month, I was enrolled at Paramount High School in Boligee, Alabama. This school was a combination of grade levels kindergarten through twelfth grade. It was one long hallway, a lunchroom, a gym, and a band room. Everyone had to cluster up in the same school.

This experience of relocation was a challenge to me because I was once again introduced to the unknown. I looked for the worse and hoped for the best. Even though I couldn't see what was happening and I didn't understand what was taking place, while the devil thought he was messing, God was already blessing. While the devil thought he was messing with my life and my divine purpose, God was already blessing my life in the midst of my mess. No! I'm not going to lie and say that it all felt good, but I will say that somehow, someway, it worked out for my good. Unknowingly, through it all, the Lord had considered my insecurities, and said, "I want you for my glory."

Chapter 6
A Shocking Experience

At this point of my life, I realized that Someone supernatural was on my side and I'm not talking about my grandmother, even though she was always there. Things began to happen for me and it seemed like they would just fall out of the sky. Boligee, Alabama was like oil and water compared to Jasper, Alabama. Jasper, Alabama was huge and rapid while in comparison to Boligee, Alabama which was small and slow. I'd never been to such a "countrified" atmosphere in my life. I was like "Oh my God, I've seen it at all now". I frowned at my grandmother's decision to relocate, but I must say unashamedly, I ended up loving that place. Greene County was a predominantly black county and astonishingly, mostly everything was black-owned. I believe that if you want to see a sea of black people who are not incarcerated, they are hid in Greene County.

Those people showed me spectacular love, which I could not receive because I was so concentrated on negativity. Those country black people loved Jesus and they were so good to me. They were always concerned about me and were very willing to assist me in whatever I needed. Yes, the curiosity about my appearance was still there, but I grew to learn this was the major part of the package of being alive. Everyone I crossed desired to know what happened to my face.

I could never forget my first day at Paramount Jr. High School. Everybody was turning their necks to gaze at me and this created an overwhelming sense of nervousness for me. Imagine that! I had a paranoid feeling like no one other. I felt worse than someone on the run from the police. Whew! I could not have been any happier when my first day at Paramount High was finally over. Amazingly, I endured those first few days of school. There is always something about those first few days of school, isn't it? They were so devastating and challenging for me.

I enrolled at Paramount Junior High School in the eighth grade. Doors began to open for me in all kinds of ways. It was unbelievable, yet still I didn't realize that Jesus was on my side. I was faced with so many opportunities and many people desired to take me in as their own.

My school year was great, but periodically, "G-THANG" would attempt to arise. I started to get in petty trouble, nothing major, just small, stupid things. The people saw great potential in me and continued their best to motivate me to be a bright kid. God was inserting great individuals in my life that had a loving and sacrificial heart in spite at my foolishness. Even though I socialized and made friends in Boligee, my grandmother was still in my life very richly. I kept phone contact with Acey and Ashley, they were thrilled at the testimonies I shared with them, and they would continue to encourage me as well.

In time however and sadly, "G-THANG" took complete control of me. I found myself gravitating to the crowds that were affiliated in the same gang I was in. Together we started terrorizing the place. After a list of small illicit escapades, I decided to do something huge, which landed me in the arms of Jesus. Surprisingly and supernaturally, my trouble was a set-up for a spectacular blessing.

My friend and I stole a vehicle and joy rode around the town of Eutaw as if it were our vehicle. With a young immature mentality, getting caught was the last thing on my mind. I was elated to be driving a vehicle. I'd go to other friend's houses and boast about how I came up. I drove to many occasions such as clubs, activity centers, and high school games. They would give me ovations on the nice vehicle, but they didn't know that it was stolen. As a youngster, I dug in the deepest trench to receive that type of notoriety. I wanted people to see me in a completely different way than I saw myself. I was a good boy at school and around my family, but at night, I was a hoodlum. Eventually my sins found me out and I was captured at the most embarrassing place ever, the store.

I was incarcerated with the big boys at the Greene County Jail. As a juvenile, I couldn't remain in the county jail, so I was transported from Greene County in Eutaw, Alabama to the Hale County Jail in Greensboro, Alabama. There I was introduced to an individual by the name of Jesus Christ. A minister from Greensboro, Alabama would come to visit all the teenagers at the detention center. I must have stood out to him in the prophetic realm because he began to prophesy over my life stating, "Young man, I don't know your name, but you're a diamond in the eyes of the lord. You're a chosen vessel and the Lord desires to use you dynamically." Even though I didn't comprehend what he had told me, I knew that I was THE CHOSEN ONE.

That same minister gave me my first Holy Bible. It was a burgundy leather Bible with my name engraved in the bottom right-hand corner. Back then, it really meant something to a person to have their name engraved on anything let alone a Bible. About two weeks following that occasion, I was transferred from Hale County Detention Center to an intense boot camp that was in Prattville, Alabama called the H.I.T. program. This camp was a temporary servitude of twenty-eight days. Those few days seemed forever. We'd have to awake at 2:00 a.m. to perform an hour of physical training. Afterwards, we ate breakfast, take a two-minute shower that was closely monitored and timed, and sit Indian style on the outside of our bedroom door the rest of the day. That was so miserable! If I dared to fall asleep, I would be "written up" but humorously, many times I would doze off to sleep because I would be so exhausted from being up at 2 am. I chose to take a write-up and go to sleep daily, but for some riveting reason, God's favor was on me in the midst of me falling asleep or you can say breaking the rules. It was a very bad situation that worked out for my good.

I learned a lot there and people saw God's favor in my life. They'd always inform me that I wasn't who I pretended to be and also encourage me that God had a plan for my life. This would leave me dazed because I knew deeply that this was what I was truly a pretender. After those twenty-eight days of camp, I was released in the summer of 1999. I went back to my grandmother's house in Boligee, Alabama. Yes, I opposed this place, but after being locked away, I grew to fall in love with the horses, and cows. After my release, everything began to go well until I chose to congregate with those same corruptible individuals. Things only got worse and I found myself being expelled from school. I blossomed as a ruffian and was a huge burden to my grandmother. I need to say that my grandmother was a very strong woman. God blessed me to have a lady of unconditional love in my corner. She put up with a lot of my foolishness. When my uncles said, "No", she'd say "Yes." In the midst of my chaotic dilemmas, people would still crown me by telling me of the good they saw in me. I found it to be strange that I could look into the mirror myself and see the same me and others could look at me and see a different me. That's amazing, isn't?

It was like the more horrific I became, the greater the love grew from the people who reminded me of the potential they saw in me. Everywhere I went, I stood out. I figured that it was my facial appearance, but it was the hand of God that people saw on me. One particular night, I was at a Greene County High School game and the individual that I rode with ended up purposely leaving me there with no ride home. It was so cold and the temperature seemed to be dropping continuously. Pride wouldn't allow me to ask for a ride home so I remained at the high school. The high school was approximately ten miles from my grandmother's house and after the games were over, I began walking in the freezing cold weather from Eutaw, Alabama to Boligee, Alabama.

I think I may have walked a mile or two when I noticed a burgundy Ford Contour creeping by me very slow. The person driving the vehicle seemed so concerned and kept looking back at me while driving. Other drivers had passed me in their vehicles who knew exactly who I was but because of my lifestyle and reputation, they did not stop to offer me a ride, so they'd only blow their horns and keep going. Yet while the other people would pass me by, the individual in the burgundy Ford Contour decided to stop and offer me a ride.

I thought to myself, "It's so cold out here, and I could use this ride", and then pride said, "Even though my ears were frozen, my hands were like an icicle and my feet felt as if I was standing in the Antarctic all day, I was straight. I didn't need a ride!" When the individual approached me in his vehicle he asked me, "Young man, where are you going this time of night?

Didn't I just see you earlier at the high school?" I answered, "Yes, I was at the high school earlier. I'm just walking to catch fresh air". You know as well as I did that I was in desperate need of a ride home. This was around midnight when this occurred. After a moment of conversation, the cold breeze forced me to get into the vehicle cautiously.

As we were riding down the road, this individual introduced himself to me as Pastor Michael A. Barton.

Pastor Barton (left) & Demetrius P Guyton (right)

Pastor Barton was the pastor of Little Zion Baptist Church in Boligee, Alabama. I noticed that he was a young man himself. On my way to my grandmother's house, I shared my testimony with him about my near death experience as an infant that resulted in my facial disfiguration. Afterwards, he invited me to church on the upcoming Sunday. I consented, but I didn't have a ride. In a sense, I felt obligated to attend his church because he was giving me a ride home. Nonetheless, I didn't want him to know that. He may have assumed so, but the ultimate goal was to get me in the church. Pastor Barton agreed to come to my grandmother's house to pick me up for church. From there, a change actually began to take place in my life.

The love, support, warmth, and compassion were there. That Sunday, he came to get me from my grandmother's house to take me to church. More so, with my attendance, he asked me to share my testimony with the congregation. I refused to because I was so shy to speak in front of people, therefore, I asked him to do it for me. When he got through sharing my testimony, the congregation became so elated jumping, shouting, and praising God for His awesomeness. Unknowingly, I was true evidence that the Lord is actually real. I didn't realize how powerful my life testimony was, but the people did. The church family fell in love with me very deeply and I became their son.

I met a woman who I know was sent from Heaven. Her name was Mrs. Marilyn Gibson. She was from Boligee, Alabama. This woman loved Jesus so much. She had five children of her own, but I really became her son. We began to cleave to each other very close. She began to take me places, mostly everywhere she went and people would always see me with her. I knew that she took a lot of criticism about being so close to me, but she overlooked all the critics and said, "This is my son! I don't care what you have to say about me or him". Mrs. Gibson was so sacrificial when it came to me and her love was unreal and endless. I also met a very wonderful woman named Mrs. Deossie Williams who also took me in as her own son. Later she introduced me to her family. I started to go to different places with her and she would introduce me to others by saying, "This is my son, Demetrius". I felt so whole around these people who accepted me for who I was. The Little Zion church family agreed to assist me in whatever I needed. My church family went to talk to the principal that had expelled me and he allowed me to come back to school. My church family was so much on my side and they fought earnestly for me until some changes were made.

Pastor Barton insisted on changing my thuggish identity into a casual look. I had very long hair with braids and the attire I wore, I sagged deeply. I allowed him to cut my hair. He was a barber and many people would come to him to get their haircuts. He also took his last $500.00 which was actually the money for his bills, and bought me numerous of dress shirts, slack, socks, belts, underclothes, and casual shoes. When he gave me my items that he purchased for me, he stated, "Demetrius, this is how you're going to present yourself to the public now. You're a new creature in Christ, old things are passed away, behold all things are becoming new." I replied, "That's fine with me."

I started to fall in love with the new me. I'd be the only one dressing casual every day at school. I'd get bright compliments from everyone. They'd say, "Boy, where have you been? What's going on here? You mean to tell me that "G-THANG" is dressing up now! There must be a living God!" I began to be very faithful at church. I know, you are probably saying I had no choice because the Pastor Barton was picking me up, but truthfully, it wasn't like that at all. It was in my heart to change, so I had to motivate myself, even when the old man desired to arise. God always kept individuals around me to keep me to make sure that I was in line.

Eventually, my grandmother saw a brand new grandson. She was so proud of me and she made a quality decision to allow me to be a part of my Little Zion Baptist Church family. I enjoyed this so much that I asked my grandmother could I dwell with Pastor Barton. She responded, "Baby, if this keeps you out of trouble then yes you can". Pastor Barton only stayed ten miles from my grandmother in Eutaw, Alabama. Even though my grandmother was very over-protective of me, she wasn't intimidated by my relocation. So I moved in with Pastor Barton and remained faithful in church and in school.

Pastor Barton assisted me in getting my first job, which was at Southfresh Processing Plant in Eutaw, Alabama. My job was to stack boxes that had already been processed. I enjoyed my job greatly. At the same time, my educational accomplishments extended to the eleventh grade. I played football and basketball for the school a few years, but mainly football. I was a quarterback. I played football for Paramount Jr. High School Bobcats in Boligee, Alabama and later went onto Greene County High, which was in Eutaw, Alabama. That went well for me, but I had no desire to pursue my quarterback career. I had gotten scout's attention from the University of North Alabama located in Florence, Alabama, University of West Alabama located in Livingston, Alabama, and Alabama A&M located in Huntsville, Alabama.

I was unable to pass the Alabama Exit Exam; therefore, I could not graduate with my class. This led me to try to get a GED. I enrolled at Concordia College GED courses in Selma, Alabama. I tried many times to earn my GED, but for some reason, I couldn't. I was still relentless at my occupation. One day while at work I experienced an unprecedented encounter of mental warfare. I couldn't explain it; nonetheless, it drove me crazy. One side of my mind was whispering, "Quit this job and go back to selling drugs! "The other side of my mind screamed, "You can do this job!

Stay strong! Don't let this blessing go!" Suddenly I heard a yell in the back of my mind yelling, "Go man! This ain't worth all of your troubles!" I allowed my mind to play tricks on me and succumbed to the bad advice from my carnal mind. So, Friday, after I got off work, I walked to the Jr. Food Mart store in Eutaw, Alabama to cash my check. After cashing my check, I stood in front of the store and waited for a ride to come to the store so I could get to my grandmother's house on the farm. The reason so was to inform her that I had a great desire to go back to Jasper, Alabama. From 3:00pm to around 8:30 or 9:00pm, I stood in front of the gas station hoping a ride would come. I still smelled like a fish plant and I had my duffle bag with me that possessed my working supplies. Finally, I noticed a blue Pontiac 6000 arrive at the gas pump. When the men got out of the vehicle, I realized that they were drug addicts. My conscience said, "If I offer them some money, they'll be willing take me to Jasper Alabama." So, I waited on them to come out of the store. Eventually they came out with a plastic bag of fifty-cent beers. Before the two men got in their vehicle, I cautiously asked them, "Hey, can I pay you to take me to Boligee, Alabama?" They agreed to take me to Boligee, Alabama to my grandmother's house, but before I went there, I asked them to stop over Pastor Barton's house, so I could get my clothes. They did so and I noticed that Pastor Barton wasn't there, but I had an extra key to his house. Before we arrived, I was in the backseat with complete strangers, yet I didn't know how to reject my mind's advice. It had me in a confusing state. I really didn't want to be in the vehicle with these strangers, but the streets of Jasper, Alabama were calling for me, and I had to get there.

SchoolDays

Chapter 7
I Thought I Had It All Figured Out

I hurriedly confiscated my property hoping that Pastor Barton didn't arrive before I was through. Without the slightest thought of why I was doing what I really didn't want to do, I finally finished packing my property. I left a note on the bed letting Pastor Barton know that I was gone. As I was writing the letter, tears leaped from my eyes drenching the note wet with my tears. I left it there in that fashion hoping that he'll notice the tears, also hoping that he noticed that I was doing something that I really didn't want to do or understand why. After minutes of an emotionally personal period, I "manned up" and got into the addict's vehicle. They took me to my grandmother's house and on the way there, I grew the boldness to ask them for a ride from Boligee, Alabama to Jasper, Alabama.

I offered them $40.00 ($20.00 apiece). Amazingly they replied, "Youngster, why are you letting something so good slip away? The preacher is taking care of you and keeping you straight and you want to leave that." Tears began to roll down my eyes and I replied to them, "I'm sorry, but you wouldn't understand if it I explained it to you. You are only looking on the outside but you are not feeling my pain. I got to go! Can you please get me away?"

These were total strangers to me because I never saw these men before, but apparently, they were seeing me with Pastor Barton. He was well respected, renowned, and adored assisting others in whatever area necessary, but I was fighting a fight internally that I couldn't explain at all. I only knew that I had to go. It was as if I had left something very valuable in Jasper, Alabama. I had to go desperately. Amazingly, they stated, "O.K. If this is what you want, let's go." We rode and conversed for a moment. I gave them direction to my grandmother's house and when we made it there I explained to her that I was going to go back to Jasper, Alabama. She was very mystified when I told her I couldn't make it in Boligee, Alabama anymore.

I looked her in her teary eyes and said, "I'm sorry mama, but I got to go. I love you so much. I just want to take care of you and I can't do it down here." She stood in the living room in such a befuddled state of manner. I hated seeing her like that. She tried repeatedly to explain to me that I didn't have to leave, but I rebelled against her response, gave hear a $100.00 bill, hugged her, kissed her on her jaw, and left. Being my grandmother and my mother, she continued to do what an average mother would do, and that was trying to change my direction. The more she tried to embrace me, the more I desired to leave.

I left the inside of her trailer, and each step I took to the vehicle, I thought to myself, "God, please keep my grandmother for me. Help her see my motive and fully understand what I was doing. Before I entered into the vehicle, I turned around once more to notice her standing on the front porch with tears streaming from her eyes. I also was very teary-eyed. For the last time, she stated, "Demetrius, baby you don't have to do this. You have a home here with me. This is why I relocated from Jasper, Alabama to give you a new outlook and beginning and you mean to tell me that you desire to go back." I looked at her with a stare of regret and replied, "Mama, you don't understand!"

I loved her dearly and adored the life I was currently living, but my mind had me in a spider web of confusion. As I got into the backseat of the vehicle, my grandmother was watching me with tears in her eyes repeatedly saying, "Baby, I love you!" I just looked back at her and gave her the longest stare as if I would never see her again. The men were convicted by the emotional conversation that my grandmother and I shared. Therefore, they tried to get me to stay, but I was filled with so much pressure, I forced them to crank up the vehicle to get me to Jasper, Alabama expeditiously.

They took my grandmother's side and tried to encourage me to stay with her, but I'd only get angry and demand to leave. They attempted many times to give me my money back also. Finally, after a brief episode of transition from a boy to a man, my uncles came outside with a huge attitude towards me and out of frustration, they told my grandmother, "Don't worry about it! Quit crying! Let him go! He'll be back! Let him hit his head against the wall a few times, I guarantee you that he'll be back here. "

After that moment, I finally persuaded the men to leave my grandmother's yard and take me to Jasper, Alabama. On the entire trip, I was perplexed and contemplated on where I was going to actually live. I had a sea of family members up there, but pride wouldn't allow me to ask them for a place to stay, especially if I just showed up without notifying them of my arrival. The trip was extremely quiet and questionable on my behalf. My travel companions would ask me countless questions, but I remained silent until we made it to Walker County. The reason I spoke to them then was that I had to give them direction to Jasper, Alabama. While I was giving them direction, I was still confused at where I was going to reside.

After deep thought, I came up with the idea that I could possibly live with my aunt, my grandmother's youngest sister. I recapped the prior years of support from her and I thought to myself that if no one accepts me, she would. I gave the men the direction to her house. We finally arrived there around 11:30 p.m. and I knocked on the door. When I knocked on the door my grandmother's sister screamed, "Who is it?" I said, "Your nephew, Demetrius!" She replied, "O.K. Come in!" I went in the house and my aunt hugged me and told me to sit down on her couch so we could talk.

I informed her of what I was doing and asked her for a place to stay. She quickly replied, "Demetrius, you know you can stay here." So, I got all of my property out of the vehicle. I introduced the driver and his associate to my aunt as I was bringing my property in the house. My aunt gave me a room with only two dressers, a radio and a closet. There was no bed or mattress at all. I had to sleep on the brown carpet that lay on the floor. My aunt and her granddaughter, my little cousin were the only two individuals that lived in the house. So I had to fix up the room myself. I offered my aunt $50.00 per week to assist her on the bills and the rent. She was fine with that.

In the meantime, my last check was at South Fresh Processing Plant in Eutaw, Alabama and I needed to pick it up, but I had no way back. So, I called one of Pastor Barton's church members, and explained to them that I needed their assistance to get to Eutaw to pick up my check. They purchased a round-trip bus ticket for me so I could travel by greyhound bus to pick up my last check. I didn't let many people see me at all. My grandmother didn't even see me. I was in and out, as a matter of fact, I walked around in the desolate area all day and night until the next day came when I could get on the bus to go back to Jasper, Alabama.

When I made it back to my aunt's house, I immediately went job searching. I called Acey and he took me to the job placement center where I put in many applications. I finally was hired at Marshall Durbin. This poultry plant was only two blocks away from my aunt's residence. I was hired as a live hanger. A live hanger's responsibility was to hang chicken on shackles while they were still alive so they could go through the boiler to be processed. This job was so disgusting and I hated it, but I had to do something to survive, therefore, I dealt with it for almost a year.

My job was close to my aunt's residence so I rode my cousin's ten-speed bicycle to work. It's a humorous thing now when I rewind that part of life in my mind. I'd ride the bicycle to work and park it in the parking spaces with the other vehicles as if it was an actual vehicle. Well, I guess you can say at that moment it was my vehicle. It was taking me where I needed to go and that was to work and back home. I'd be in the break room at work and comments would fly through the air. People would say, "Who in their lost mind rode a bicycle and parked it in the parking space?" I'd be quiet as a mouse and still as a rock.

After work, I'd stay back for hours until everyone that was parked in the parking lot would depart. Then I'd get in my vehicle, or on the bicycle and drive off. Eventually, after a few days, they found out who was riding the bicycle and parking it in the parking lot. Me! People laughed at me about that for a long, long time. Days of mockery passed and an individual with a compassionate heart to ask me, "Hey, do you want me to come pick you up for work and take you back home?" Pridefully, I said, "No I'm straight!" They finally convinced me into saying "Yes, I'll take the ride."

One particular night, I went to a popular nightclub that my uncle owned in Jasper, Alabama called "Shakers". There, I met a woman who I innocently thought was going to be the entirety of my life. She was much older than I was, approximately ten years older to be candid. I actually felt genuine and comfortable about this. After only six months of knowing each other, we got married.

Being only sixteen years old, this was the most amazing and devastating time of my life. On that day when I said, "I do", I knew I had to make a complete 180^0 turn in my life. I called my friends and my family to inform them that I had gotten married. My friends were elated, but my family was disturbed. For a while, I was confused because I thought that if anyone would be happy would have been my family. They thought that it was a foolish decision and my grandmother would say, "Baby, you're too young to be talking about being married." Truthfully, I was, but I was gratified by the love that was seemingly shown to me. I loved my family with my all, but I never understood that being married meant to be totally changed. I continued to be the normal teenager. I'd seek confidential counseling from my friends that were married and had been married for years trying to find out what I needed to do to keep my marriage alive and blossoming, but the advice that they gave me was like Chinese language to me.

I couldn't see how and why she could find me to be so special in her eyes. It was as if a veil was over my eyes and all of this was so unreal. I would call Acey occasionally and inform him of this and he would only say, "Demetrius this means that it's time for you to chill out from the streets and get in the house".

We rented an old 1970's grayish blue brick house from an individual that was considered the wealthiest man in Winfield, Alabama. The Lord had given us awesome favor to be able to give him five hundred dollars for the first month and deposit. We were completely moved in the house in two days and it was livable. Her mother had given us furniture that she had stored in an old trailer that she had isolated in an area on which they possessed a bit of land. Actually, this was the trailer were they grew up. This was so stunning to me because this was the first house that I could actually call home. I had my own keys to a house and I was looked at as the head of our house. Many teenagers desired to be in my shoes. People were overwhelmed at this and truthfully, so was I. I was like "Whoa!" I'm a husband, step-father, and son-in-law. I needed to know how to carry myself. I didn't want to camouflage the real me, a befuddled guy, but I had to do something quick because the camera was on me. There were many questions that I had to ask, but it seemed like no one could understand me let alone give me answers to my questionings. Moreover, I found myself multiplying my character. I would change completely depending on my atmosphere. Around my wife, stepchildren, and my mother-in-law, I was this nice, strong, and dependable guy, but around the fellows, I was "G-THANG."

Confusion bombarded my mind, I was in a jam, and eventually, pride would push me away from my counselors. I relocated from Jasper, Alabama to Winfield, Alabama to be with my family. Seeking advice was not an option because I thought I had it all figured out.

I sought work all over Winfield, Alabama and the Marion County areas, but there was no luck. Guess what! Money had to come in real quick as I was slapped in the face with so many responsibilities. It seemed as if I couldn't catch air anywhere. I was running through muddy waters trying to find dry land. After all the nagging about bills, rent, and groceries, etc., I realized that marriage wasn't my cup of tea. Between the battles of my mind, the fellows, and the household, I cleaved to the fast lane of life again.

When I privately jumped into the streets to provide for my family, I must say, unashamedly I started to meet the needs of my house. Spontaneously, my wife's family began to spy my every move. What's a guy like me supposed to do once the family began to get in the mix? This was so frustrating once I came to the knowledge of this. I thought very deeply to leave but I couldn't because my heart wouldn't let me. Therefore, I had to get it or die trying. I got so notorious secretly that people would begin to be intimidated by me. I'd do vicious things to earn money to take care of my family. I got money in the streets without my family knowing it. I did a good job at blending in with the forests, and trees, until the light exposed the dark. That's very embarrassing when the light shines in the darkness of your foolishness. Needless to say, my foolishness had been revealed and it seemed like it caught me on the blindside.

I was arrested and taken in to the Marion County Jail in Hamilton, Alabama. I was still unlearned of God's grace and mercy, but I did see that something supernatural was on my side. I was charged with counts of drugs possession and distribution, but somehow, the charges were dropped. In my carnal mind I thought I was doing or had done something great, but I learned it was nothing about me. Due to my temporary servitude at the Marion County Jail, negative criticism would scatter all over and people would tell my family that I was no good and to get rid of me.

I had an awesome family. My wife was very compassionate and devoted to me regardless of the chatter from the people, but I was still blind. Yes, I was so blind to what meant the world to me, my family. In my family's eyes, I was everything, but in my own eyes, I was nothing. While I was in the county jail, I had time to see myself and realize that this wasn't really me at all. Many people told me this, but I guess I had to learn the hard way.

The following Thursday after my incarceration, a guy named Mr. Burr Franks from Winfield, Alabama came to the county jail to minister to us. As he was speaking, it seemed as if he was talking directly to me. I was very convicted by the word that the Lord had imparted to him. After service, he prophesied over me and stated that God had chosen me to be a great man of the kingdom. Truthfully, I was confused because I couldn't see that God desired to use me for His glory. Anyone but me, anyone but me I thought. That prophetic message stuck with me for a while like a leech on an animal's skin. The following Thursday when Mr. Franks came back to the county jail and held a baptism service I got baptized in a blue fifteen foot long bucket in the shower. By the thunderous lifestyle I was living, it was so unbelievable to the individuals on the outside that had heard about it.

On the Sunday visitation when my wife came to see me, I informed her that I had been baptized and she hollered to the top of her lungs, "What!" You should have seen the facial expression on the other visitors and officers. She hollered as if I had told her that I had been sleeping with her best friend. I had to explain her holler to the officers and the other visitors by replying to their confused and questioning expressions that my wife was excited that I had gotten baptized. That comforted them and they continued their visit. It was so humorous! My wife spread the news of my baptism abroad, but the people doubted my sincerity and would tell her, "He's only doing that because he desires to be out of jail". She had many arguments trying to defend my decision as an earnest sincere life change. Eventually I told her that those arguments were not worth having because people would think what they wanted to no matter what.

I remained in the county jail for only two months, but those two months took forever to expire. I was convicted and given a three-year probationary period, which was only twelve to fourteen months to serve. I still didn't know anything about those inseparable twins called grace and mercy. I did realize that I was blessed beyond belief, because others with lesser cases than mine would get much stiffer sentences and yet I got a slap on the wrist. When I was freed, people would act as if I was the most vicious person alive, but actually, I was free as a bird. I was so unlearned to spiritual warfare and the battles my mind would face. The enemy took full advantage of that and began to come at me cruelly.

I did as Mr. Franks told me, found myself in a good church, and joined myself with good Christian people. Everyone carnal would criticize my decision of a changed life. This was a fight like never before. I was like "Wow! If being a Christian would mean dealing with all of this, then maybe I should've stayed being the ruffian that I was." My Wife was still being a faithful wife to through it all. A year or so later, we were blessed to receive a three bedroom doublewide trailer that had two bathrooms. When this blessing occurred, my bottom lip dropped to my feet.

Our trailer was in Hamilton, Alabama, which was twenty miles approximately from Winfield, Alabama where we previously lived. I moved very anxiously hoping that the relocation would detour and/or deviate the drama from the people. I also hoped that this would refurbish our marriage and household. The move was great and successful, but the enemy was dedicated to attack my household and me. It was amazing and painful at the same time, because this was the beginning of an ending marriage.

Chapter 8
No Pain, No Gain

Repeatedly, people would insist on informing me that all of my foolish ways were going to come to a halt and when it did, it was as if I had been jinxed. They say when it rains it pours, but in my case, when it rained, it was a tsunami. All kinds of crazy things begin to shuffle towards my direction. My whole world seemed to be turning upside down before my very eyes. I had everything that a teenager dreamed of. I had along with my family, two mobile homes, three vehicles, and a lot of money, and other miscellaneous. Yet and still, there was a vehement void.

My wife and I would find ourselves in immature arguments and other things led to an incompatibility in our relationship. This led me to seek love somewhere else, because I felt as if my presence was synthetic. So, I made up in my mind that I was going to find someone to love and accept me for me, not knowing that my family really did love me all the while, it was just me tripping. It seemed too good to be true.

She'd would tell me constantly, "Baby, I love you. I need you. I also trust you. In times of insecurities, I lean on your shoulder." This blew my mind! I was like, "Who me? I know you're not telling me that you love me, need me, and trust me!" She replied with a grin, "Yes, I love you. You're my everything." I didn't it say to her, but I was seeking for the same thing. She found security in me. It was so attractive to me and I couldn't resist her love at all. I've had many relationships before but none like this.

I'd always say to God, "Please, don't let me blow this one this time. I've messed up every other opportunity, but I don't need to mess this one up. At times when we would be alone I would tell her, "You saved my life when you married me". She'd just smile very joyously, but she really didn't understand the real content behind what I told her. When I would be with her, the children, and her mother, I'd contemplate on where I'd be if I were not with them. I would have probably been dead, in prison, or maybe so entangled in the streets that it would have taken something dynamic to pull me out.

Periodically, I felt the love that we once shared scaling away. The concerns and support was slim, the atmosphere started to get dim and the interest and zeal that we once had started to fade away and I found myself cheating. After I'd be intimate with the other women, I'd be torn apart with tears of regret. I was sinking in sand deeper and deeper than I could ever imagine. Once again, couldn't anyone feel my uncontrollable and unexplainable pain? The other women would question my confusion, but I'd only be confidential and act as if it was all good when I really felt bad.

Finally, after the rubber met the road, she came out with the breaking news, "Demetrius, I don't think that I could do this anymore." I screamed in anguish, "What! This can't be! What's going on?" I knew all the while that this time would eventually come. I was in a daze but this was really it. I had blown it! I had the worst grudge against God because I asked him in sincerity not to let me blow this one, and supposedly, I thought He did. I tried relentlessly to salvage my marriage, but no luck. Nothing mattered anymore at all about anything to me. I didn't understand life and my purpose of being born.

There were a lot of questions, but I dared not to ask God. Because I was told never to question Him and that He knew how to work it out. My wife was my heart inside of heart. I thought that I couldn't make it in life without my family. The best thing I ever had was going down the drain and I knew I had to do whatever it took to win my family back in my life. I'd duck and dodge my family and friend's advice, even though I knew deeply that they were so right about everything. All that I had settled in my mind was to get back what belonged to me.

THE CHOSEN ONE TOUCH FROM ABOVE

I was downtrodden about this for months. This literally dragged me down to the lowest part of my life. I'm very grateful that I didn't stoop as low as using and shooting drugs. Drugs were always a thing that I'd reject, simply because I saw what it did to others. I couldn't stand drugs and its results. Sad to say, I sold it to feed my family and to support me financially. As I looked at myself and weighed out the situation, I saw myself actually going down. My attitude, conduct, and character had been demoted.

One day, I was riding in my vehicle trying to gather myself, and something spectacular happened. As I stopped at a red light, a thought was inserted into my mind very heavily directing me to go to the Bevill State Community College in Hamilton, Alabama. I responded to the heaviness of my mind. I was clueless why I was impressed to go to this place. I turned left when the light changed from red to green still with no understanding of why was I really going to the Bevill State Community College.

When I went into this college, I met a lady named Mrs. Adine Kimbrough. Mrs. Kimbrough was an employee at the Hamilton Career Center that was adjoined to the Bevill State Community College. Her occupation was to assist jobless people to find jobs. I sat at her desk and asked her to help me find a job. Getting a job, I thought, would regain trust and loyalty from my family. Not knowing and understanding that the better I was trying to become, the worse it seemed like things grew. So, Mrs. Kimbrough asked me some very personal questions that blew my mind. I began to open myself to her as if I had known her for years.

I told her what I was dealing with because I felt so comfortable around her, even though this was my first time meeting this lady. She gave me awesome advice, and at the same time, she was getting things together to get off work. Mrs. Kimbrough began to tell me about her husband who had been in servitude in the Alabama Department of Corrections and is now a pastor. I desired so greatly to meet this man. She allowed me to follow her to their residence from the college.

Amazingly, their house was only a block away from the trailer where we lived. When I arrived at their house, I noticed her husband sitting on the front porch waiting patiently as if he was expecting me to come. Mrs. Kimbrough introduced us to each other and went into the house. He interestingly asked me, "What's up?" I said, "Pastor Kimbrough, I'm stuck between a rock and a hard spot." Pride began to speak to my mind saying,

"He ain't going to listen to you. He doesn't understand your issues. This is a huge waste of time. You're not even on his level. You're not important enough to be in their yard, let alone being on their porch."

My desperation for advice and my mind had a great battle, but I overcame my mental wars. I was desperately determined to figure out my purpose of me being at their house and the reason I was led to the college. We opened up in a word of prayer and in the prayer; it was as if he was dialoguing with the Lord about me. Inwardly, I was like, "Whoa, this man knows something." After the prayer, I began to be comfortable and open with him much like my conversation with Mrs. Kimbrough at the college.

When it appeared to me that I could be real with him, I got really personal with him. I also recollected the information that Mrs. Kimbrough told me about him being an ex-felon. That alone told me that he had not been saved all of his life. So, I figured I could fully lay it all out on the table. Even though he was Pastor of the Greater New Beginning Baptist Church in Hamilton, Alabama, I still recognized that he was human just like me.

All of a sudden, he spoke to me as if he was a mind reader saying, "Young man, you can be real with me, I've been there and done that, so I can sympathize with you completely". Then I asked him "What's a man? How does a man carry himself?" I thought that this was the most embarrassing questions that an individual could ever ask, but I learned that this was a common question that lost, confused and desperate men ask secretly on the inside. He replied, "Demetrius, a man is a person who does the will of God and handles his responsibilities of the family."

He explained to me the will of God and how I needed to go about aligning my will with God's will. We dialogued for quite a while we had to cut our conversation short because Pastor Kimbrough had to go to his Wednesday night Bible study. He invited me to the Bible study at his church and I consented. So we postponed our conversation until after Bible study. I left my vehicle in their yard and rode with them. The study was so profound because it coincided with my issues.

When we arrived back at their house, Pastor Kimbrough and I went into the living room and had a heart to heart discussion. I was concentrating on his advice greatly because he was feeding my mind's stomach. He related to my separation, my abnormal thinking and my perpetually perplexed mind. After conversing with him, I knew I had to get my act together. I had to maneuver very quickly because my all was slowly slipping away from my hands. So after receiving the invitation to go to their church I began to be faithful and dedicated.

I started to take my family along with me to church every Sunday. I'd also ask my wife if she wanted to come along with us, but pride wouldn't let her. It seemed like the enemy was attacking me in all areas that I was trying earnestly to fulfill, I began to pray in the house and asked my household to join me, but they would only laugh at me as if they didn't care at all. This seemed so crazy to me and I was on the edge to lay this Christian life down.

Somehow, I had the nerve to get into my vehicle and go to Pastor Kimbrough's house and explain to him what was going on. I told him that this was very crazy and I needed to know what was going on. I also asked him, "Was all this worth all the hell I'm going through?" It seemed like things were a little bit better before I desired to do the right thing. My wife and I were the happiest people before I desired to do right. When I laid the old man aside, all hell began to break loose. Persecution was coming from everywhere, simply because of the decision I had made.

I was so overwhelmed by the attacks that were coming at me and I was ignorant to the spiritual nature of this warfare. Every time persecution, hate, slander, ostracizing, and criticism started to come my way, I'd call Pastor Kimbrough or go to his house to get some advice. He always told me that for Christians, this persecution was motivation. To me, it was humiliation. I'd repeatedly ask Pastor Kimbrough, "How in the world could my trials and tribulations be defined as "motivation?" It seemed to be more devastating than anything as my whole world seemed to tumble upside down. Yet Pastor Kimbrough insisted that this was "motivation" for the children of God.

I was lost and in need of a clearer definition of my afflictions. After the conversation, I vacated their premises with the word "motivation" on my mind and in my spirit. I was also trying to figure out how I could use this word "motivation" to my advantage. It was really pulling on my mental coattail. Meanwhile, I was still confused trying to figure out this denuding dilemma. Determination and dedication were engraved in my heart in pursuing to plow my broken marriage, but hope was seemingly hopeless.

I went to a car lot and purchased a white 1993 Buick Park Avenue. We had a vehicle but it was in my mother-in-law's, name and if anything didn't go right between US she would take it. Therefore, I desired to have my own vehicle.

On March 16, 2005, something so incomprehensible happened to me while on my way to Pastor Kimbrough's church for a Wednesday night Bible study. I wasn't aware that he had to make an urgent trip to Pennsylvania, so there was no service that night.

There was an individual that I made drug deals with who owed me $50.00 so I decided to visit this person on his job at JR Food Mart and Gas Station in Hamilton, Alabama. So after leaving the church I decided to stop by the store to ask this individual for my money.

When I asked this individual for my money, they told me that they didn't have it. When I told them that I was low in gas, they told me that I could get some gas (JR Food Mart also sold gasoline) to put in my vehicle. So I filled my vehicle up which came to $31.51. I thanked the individual and informed them that I was done getting the gas. I also told them not to worry about the rest of the money they owed me. I had enough gas to make it to my job. This person replied, "O.k. Have a great night."

I left with a comfortable feeling of thinking that this was an official sale but to my surprise as I was on Highway 17 on my way back to the trailer I was pulled over by the Hamilton City Police. I was calm, cool, and collected because I felt that I had not done any wrong. I actually thought that I was being pulled over because I didn't have an official tag on my vehicle because my vehicle had a temporary dealership tag on it, as I had not yet purchased a tag. To my dismay, the individual that allowed me to get the gas had called the police on me and falsely informed them that I had stolen the gas.

When the officer approached my vehicle, I had my driver's license and other paperwork in my hand to exhibit to him, but it wasn't necessary. He asked, "Mr. Guyton, did you just leave the Jr. Food Mart?" I replied, "Yes, Sir." He brought it to my attention that my vehicle was the description of a gas theft drive off. I was so mind blown at this. I was given the rotten end of the stick. Nonetheless, I remained quiet about the previous transaction that the individual and I had previously done at the Jr. Foodmart gas station.

The officer asked me to follow him to the store to settle the matter. For some reason, I knew that I was going to go back to the county jail behind this. I was honest in trailing him to the store, even I was quite angry over the betrayal. There were so many ways that I could've vanished. As soon as he pulled off, two more vehicles came between us on the highway. My flesh was telling me, "Demetrius, punch the gas and keep going!" I was less than a mile away from my house and I could have lost the officer, but I desired to do the right thing. Man! What a temptation!

The enemy was really speaking to my mind saying, "Go Demetrius, you got him!" I truly did have him, but my heart wouldn't let me mash the gas. I had to be as honest as I could in this in devastating dilemma. Consciously, I contemplated on whether I was going to be transported to the Marion County Jail from where I had just been set free in the previous month. Wow! What a mental and spiritual fight! By the assistance of the Holy Spirit, I passed the test of not fleeing.

Finally, we arrived at the store can imagine Jesus' smile being very bright at my obedience, even though he foresaw a set-up to destroy me. I often wonder if He boasted about me to the Father and to the angelic host saying, "Look at my son, in whom I'm well-pleased!" Well, I got out of my vehicle leaving it running with the windshield wipers on because it was drizzling. The officer and I went into the store to conclude this matter. As soon as I walked in the door the individual screamed, "Yes, officer that's him he done it!"

I was so bemused at this bold thing that this person had done to me. Revenge was in my veins and all I could think was that I was on my way back to jail. Still, I remained calm not knowing what was about to take place. The officer asked me for my I.D. and informed me that if I didn't have any warrants on me, I could have the opportunity to call someone to reimburse the store, but if I had a warrant, I was going to be taken into custody. After checking my I.D., he informed me that I was free of any warrants.

Without any warrants against me, I felt sure that I had a good chance of not going to the county jail. All of a sudden, another officer came for back up. This officer was so cruel and very hateful. I believe that he was sent by Satan himself. He crashed my opportunity of being able to reimburse the $31.50 to the Jr. Food Mart and requested that I be transported to the Marion County Jail. As they tried to arrest me, I resisted greatly because I was full of rage. It was very difficult for both of the officers to subdue me because my nerves had risen to the top like a thermometer's fluid on the inside of the glass to show measurement. I was very angry.

That was one of the most embarrassing moments I have ever experienced in my life. Several individuals drove by, many who knew Pastor

Kimbrough or me. They would slow down their vehicles, roll down their windows, and say, "Demetrius, what's going on? Are you o.k.? How can we assist you? I'll tell Pastor Kimbrough that the officers have you in custody". I dreadfully shook my head in regret. I felt so pitiful and in disbelief. All I could do was just stare at the people hoping that they could paraphrase my emotions and see my answer through this. Following a five or ten minute tussle, I was finally tackled down by multiple officers and taken back to Marion County Jail where I previously confessed Christ as Lord and Savior of my life and had been baptized.

Pastor Theodis Kimbrough

Demetrius & First Lady Kimbrough

Chapter 9
Imagine Yourself In My Shoes

Man I can't believe this mess at all! I'm back in the county jail! I was so disgusted, angry, frustrated, and confused. The criticizers were waiting for this moment to occur in my life so they could say, "See, I told you that he was only perpetrating all the while". It was like an interruption of a great telecast with the breaking news moment when they found out that I had been incarcerated once again. I felt so belittled for many reasons and I couldn't think of a word to describe this degrading dilemma. I was more overwhelmed than anything because I had been falsely accused.

I negotiated with the officers pertaining to this synthetic matter. Even though this individual had falsely accused me of stealing gas, I still kept the details of my transaction with the false accuser confidential. I guess you say, "If I was him, I'd spill the beans." Well, I didn't! Truthfully, I had resentment and retaliation on my mind and in my heart towards this individual. I stated within myself that if I were to ever see this person again, I'd do something very cruel to them.

When we arrived at the Marion County Jail, the trustees, jailors, and other inmates were looking at me with such a confused and wandering stare in their eyes, shaking their heads saying aloud, "Wow! He just left and he's back already!" I would rather have been a homeless person under a bridge holding a sign of desperation advertising that I was in need rather than being incarcerated at that moment.

As I was getting out of the backseat of the Hamilton City Police car handcuffed, people from everywhere rushed up to me asking me what happened and how did I get into a position to be coming back to jail. At that moment, I could sympathize greatly with the stars that are followed by the paparazzi. Yes! That's how I felt! No comments at all! At least the stars could've covered their faces. I was handcuffed. Imagine that!

People followed me from the car to the booking room and from the booking room to the main population asking me, "How? Why? What happened?" I didn't desire dialogue with anyone at that time, not even God. When they tried to talk to me, I'd brush them off. The sheriff, jail administrator, secretaries, officers, bookkeepers, and cooks, were all in disbelief at my return so soon after my release. I wanted so badly to shut myself in a cell and just sleep my life away. I secretly tried to commit suicide many times while in the cell alone, but that didn't work at all. So I had no other choice but to face my situation head on.

Now that I look back, I see that this was a catalyst designed by God to usher me to a deeper and more dependable level in Him. I couldn't believe that all of this was meaningful, but amazingly, it was. Meanwhile, Mr. Burr Franks was continuing to come to the county jail to minister to us every Thursday. I felt as if this was one of the most embarrassing moments in my life. I got saved, baptized, and delivered from this place and there I was back again. I could never forget that night. It was on a Wednesday night, five days after my first anniversary. I can imagine all the embarrassment and criticism my wife had to endure from family and friends abroad.

The next day, Mr. Franks came to minister to us. I was very nerve wrecked at the fact that I had just left the county jail and here I was back again. My mind was telling me that I was going to look like a complete fool in his eyes. I thought that I was going to be picked out to be picked on. At 7:00 p.m. when they called "Church Call", I sprinted into my cell and closed the door feeling so miserable. When Mr. Frank's arrived in the cell block and began to speak, his voice was so deep he could speak over a speeding Mac-Truck Even closing the cell door, didn't silence his voice at all. His voice was so demanding. Even though I knew deep in my heart that I should have been in the day room along with the other guys, pride had me so entangled that I was actually terrified to join the service.

Mr. Franks began to minister out of the book of Haggai 1: 5-9. His topic was "Consider Your Ways" and it was as if he was speaking directly to me. Those words were beaming through the metal federal facility doors that had me incarcerated. Conviction would leap on me so hard that I'd actually try to stuff something in the cracks of the door and in my ears. It was wounding me to hear the word that he was preaching, not because I was rejecting it, but I was wrapped up in pride.

As he was getting ready to close and vacate the premises, I felt an ease. My pride was being relieved and relaxed on the inside. All of a sudden, I heard the guys say, "Mr. Franks, Demetrius Guyton is back!" He's in cell 27! He ran inside of his cell when they called "Church Call". I could've wrung their necks and hung them on shackles as I had done those chickens when I was hired as a live-hanger.

As I heard Mr. Frank's footsteps approaching my cell, I got under the covers and turned my head towards the wall snoring with the fakest snore ever. I hoped that he would notice me sleeping and decide to leave, but he opened the door tapped me on my shoulders. I rolled over to look at him with tears leaping out of my eyes. I grasped his coat and silently asked him, "Why? I didn't understand this at all! Why me? "He replied, "Demetrius, God has a great work for you and you are His chosen vessel. You are "THE CHOSEN ONE". He also prayed for me, shared some encouraging words with me, and expressed his love for me along with his sincere support.

Before he left, he told me, "Demetrius, you don't have to be ashamed. God loves you and I do too. I know that this may seem incomprehensible to you now, but remain strong and endure what He is allowing you to go through and will see you through it." I knew deeply that somehow, someway, this horrible and unexpected invasion would work out for my good. So, I began to consider what he told me as I explained to him what happened to me on that Wednesday night at the gas station. He informed me that he was already familiar with what went on.

Astonishingly, this man knew exactly what happened as if he was in a vehicle in a dark area or in the bushes camouflaged watching. He promised me that he'd be my arm of support through it all. After minutes of dialoguing, he left and I immediately closed my cell door, locked it, and cried out to the Lord with my all. I finally fell asleep and rested very peacefully.

When I awoke the next morning, I felt like a completely different individual. The circumstance that I was in had no effect on me anymore. What once had a hold on me I grew the strength to have a hold on it. I could actually see me doing and being exactly who God said I was. I held my head up high and begin to become very joyous and jubilant even though I was in the "Lion's Den." The other guys would ask me, "Demetrius, what is it about you? Why are you so happy?" I replied, "I'm blessed, truly blessed." Some would say, "There's a glow about you shining very brightly". I smiled with the appreciation of the confirmation that the hand of the Lord was really upon me. I was a resurrected man with a resurrected mentality.

On the following Sunday, I got a surprising visit from Pastor Kimbrough. He wasn't angry with me at all as I thought that he'd be. He was actually angry with himself because he didn't inform me that he had to make an urgent trip to Pennsylvania. He felt that if I had known better, I would have done better. I encouraged him that it wasn't his fault. It was just designed to happen this way. I truly grew an awesome confidence that God had me covered. Our visit went very well. He also encouraged me and informed me to trust Jesus in the midst of what was taking place.

My marriage was hanging by a spider's web. I asked Pastor Kimbrough along with his wife to go to my residence to minister to my wife and to help her understand that this was the Lord's doing. He and his wife did as I had requested and my wife came to see me on the next visitation. As we dialogued, she stressed to me that she was confused and had no desire to remain with me. Pastor Kimbrough intervened by sharing his testimony with us about how Mrs. Adine Kimbrough hung in there with him while he was in servitude. He also explained how it grew their love stronger.

By doing this, he tried to persuade my wife to hang on to our marriage, but she was very leery about this decision because of what it looked like instead of what it was going to be. After a few more visits from my wife, she completely ceased from doing anything. So I contemplated very hard and I concluded that when I was released, I wasn't going to have anything to do with her at all anymore. I felt like she treated me like the fifth cousin at the family reunion.

I went to my probation revocation on May 25th, 2005, with high expectations that I'd be released, but reinstatement was not granted. I was to serve my three-year probation period that I had previously received. I also had to reimburse the thirty-one dollars and fifty cents back to the Jr. Food Mart for the gas that I was falsely accused of stealing. I wanted to go home desperately, but it didn't happen that way. I remained in the county jail awaiting the trip to the penitentiary to serve my three-year sentence.

I remained in the Marion County Jail from March 16th, 2005 until August 1st, 2005. On this August day, I was called out of the population of inmates into the hallway to talk with the secretary. She informed me that I was given an opportunity to be released on house arrest. She said it in words like, "I don't know why I'm doing this, but I'm going to let you go home and serve the remainder of your time. Do you have anyone to pick you up?" I immediately screamed, "Yes I do!"

Pastor Kimbrough had a collect call block on his phone, so, I called my grandmother to inform her to relay the message to Pastor Kimbrough that I had a chance to leave and that I needed him to come pick me up. During this time, Pastor Kimbrough was in Florida and could not pick me up. The rest of the guys were so amazed that I had an opportunity to leave but could not get someone to pick me up. They'd ask me repeatedly, "Demetrius, why are you not gone yet?" I'd tell them, "I'm going to leave shortly; I'm just waiting on my family". That seemed forever! Friday came and no Pastor Kimbrough. Saturday came and no Pastor Kimbrough. Sunday came and no Pastor Kimbrough. Can you imagine me by now? I was one boiling individual. I had an opportunity to be free from jail and was stuck. How many opportunities have you had to be "FREE" but something kept you "BOUND?" What a miserable feeling that was.

I thought that the secretary would recognize that I was still there at the county jail and snatch away the opportunity for me to go home. I went to sleep thinking what I could do. The next morning, a voice awoke me from a very deep sleep screaming to the top of its lungs "Demetrius Guyton, all the way! Pack your stuff! Let's go! I quickly hopped out of the bed and sprinted up the hallway leaving everything but my Bible. Yes, I left everything. I did not even wash my face or brush my teeth.

I ran expeditiously out of population into the hallways with only a pair of boxer briefs on and a pair of socks. The officers, secretaries, cooks and other inmates were so tickled at watching me run down the hallway in to the dressing room. Do you think that I cared about what they said or thought about me? No! I didn't! Of course not! I was ready to get out of that den. I beat the officer to the laundry room where my personal belongings were.

When I opened the laundry room door, there was a trustee awaiting me. He introduced himself to me and at the same time smiling saying, "Young man, are you o.k.?" I replied, "Yeah, I am now. I'm just fine." He continued to say, "Demetrius, you may not know me but I know you. I also know that you are given another chance of freedom. Don't come here anymore. You got blessed greatly to escape the penitentiary and get to finish your time at home."

Finally, the officer arrived with great laughter at how I previously ran up the hallway with only my socks and boxer briefs on. After the officer gave me my personal belongings, I hurriedly put on my clothes, signed the release papers, and dropped the ink pen on the table with a quick instinct to leave. Suddenly, the secretary grabbed me by my arms and said, "Demetrius hold on for a minute." I looked at her with great intentions to ask her, "Woman, what in the world is up with you! Have you gone crazy! You better let my arm go so I can leave this dungeon."

Somehow I was able to discern that there was a genuine concern and she wanted me to halt, she wanted my full attention. Even though I was ready to leave, I didn't allow my mind to control my conviction. So out of curiosity I actually stopped to see what she really wanted. Let me tell you, the look that she gave me was like none other. I saw a great heartfelt caring and concern in her eyes. Unashamedly and surprisingly, the secretary looked into my eyes and began to tell me, "Demetrius, there's something very special and attractive about you. This place is not where you belong. Please don't come back here. I've given you an opportunity that others would love to have, so take advantage of it. Don't you see how it is in this place? Please don't come back here! Be the man that I see inside of you." I said, "Yes, Ma'am" with my arm still in her hands in the presence of the jailors and the bookkeepers.

Her words penetrated my heart very deeply. I began to look her into her eyes for several seconds and said, "Thank you so much for seeing someone greater than me inside of me". Afterwards, she told me, "I've been secretary here for five years and I've never talked to anyone like I have talked with you. I have great interest in you and your life. I also desire for you to be a great, productive, and dependable man. Make your loved ones happy. My response to her was a great stare along with a great big smile.

Before leaving, she said, "Demetrius, take care of yourself." I said, "O.K.", and slowly walked out of the double doors with the words of wise counsel she had injected inside of me. As I was chewing on those powerful words of advice, I looked in the parking lot and saw Pastor Kimbrough backed into the parking space with a very delighting smile on his face. He rolled down the window and said humorously, "Son, what took you so long to get out of there? "I smiled as I entered into his grey Mercury Mountaineer Jeep and explained to him what the secretary had told me.

Chapter 10
Be Real With Yourself

As I was sitting on the passenger's side of Pastor Kimbrough's jeep, I felt accepted and loved just as the prodigal son when he came back to his father's house. Pastor Kimbrough had a relentless smile on his face as I imagine the Father did in the parable of the prodigal son's return. He was so delighted to see me again and to have me near him. I humorously fussed at him saying, "What took you so long?" He explained to me that an emergency came up and he had to go to Florida. Well, I guess this was excusable! It really didn't matter because I had been released.

I was so happy to be free and to see Pastor Kimbrough on the other side of the fence. It was such a blessing to receive my physical freedom once again. I rode down the road with an internal praise enjoying every moment of the opportunity. Though I couldn't smell, I was trying to breathe in every drop of air I could. Too often people take for granted what they should be taking full advantage of. Pastor Kimbrough informed me that he was told that I had to visit my probation officer, who was in charge of the community corrections program in Winfield, Alabama.

She was a very compassionate and loving, but very direct woman. She believed in giving people another chance to get themselves together, but if you pushed her to the limit, she'd do her job. Do you blame her? Pastor Kimbrough and I went to her office. On the way there, we had a conversation like a father and son would have best. I felt so safe and secure with the warm conversation that we had and took it to heart with ultimate intentions to do as requested. When we made it to her office, she gave me an orientation and explained the obligations I had to meet. I understood my punishment very clearly, signed papers and we left on our way back to Hamilton, Alabama.

I only had one hundred and fifty feet perimeter because I had been placed on house arrest. I was only able to go to church, work and back home. Even though I was on house arrest, Pastor Kimbrough and I rode home very elated at the blessings of the Lord. Pastor Kimbrough informed me that I was a chosen vessel for the Kingdom of God. I knew that I was blessed, but I questioned how I could connect with the One who was closely monitoring me. After riding a few miles down the road, I asked Pastor Kimbrough, "Where will I be living?" I truly didn't desire to go back to my wife's trailer. I was very firm on what I had uttered to myself in the cell at the Marion County Jail.

After asking Pastor Kimbrough the question and thinking to myself, "I hope he doesn't take me back to my old residence". He replied, "Son, you're going to be living with me and my family. We've opened our door to you and we accept you as our own child." Unknowingly, he took full responsibility of me. Look at Jesus! I was so excited about this. I was happier than a child in a toy factory. I asked Pastor Kimbrough "Are you really doing this for me?" He answered, "Yes I am". My joy grew into soberness because I knew that I had to go back to my old residence to get my personal belongings. This was something that I really truly resented doing because I knew if I were to lay my eyes on my wife, the old man in me would itch to spark up reconciliation.

Being real with myself, I honestly wasn't strong enough yet to see my wife and not desire to be with her. I was really trying to be a man of my word, but I had unexplainable love in my heart for my family. My love for them was so tender and authentic. This love that I possessed was so strong, that it completely covered my intentions. Pastor Kimbrough wasn't aware of this yet because I didn't inform him, but when he said, "Demetrius, we're going to your trailer to get your stuff", I immediately shouted, No! I'll do without!" He said, "What do you mean you'll do without? You have to get your belongings." I tried justifying without delving into details by saying, "What about your son? Does he have any clothes that I can fit?" That didn't work at all. I tried repeatedly to explain to him why I didn't want to go back to my old residence.

I was so serious about this I was willing to wear the clothes that I had been wearing for several days than go back over there. Nevertheless, Pastor Kimbrough spoke life into my dead situation and it seemed like I couldn't win at all. Therefore, justifying my position wasn't a wise thing to continue doing so we went on to the trailer. The closer we got, the more I wanted to jump out of the jeep. I literally begged him not to do this, but he thought it better to go on anyway. While he was continuing to drive, my palms became very sweaty, the hairs on my neck stood up, and my nerves rattled. I felt like I was going to break.

Finally, we arrived to the trailer, but my wife was gone. I gave Pastor Kimbrough her cell phone number and he called her to inform her that we were in the yard awaiting her arrival. My trailer key was on my keychain inside the vehicle that had been towed from the Jr. Food Mart on the night of my arrest. The atmosphere around my wife's trailer was so quiet and calm that while Pastor Kimbrough was talking to her I could hear her voice so clearly as if she was actually in the yard with us. At the sound of her voice, I melted on the inside, especially when I heard her say, "I'll be there shortly".

When he hung up the phone, we mingled around the yard talking and awaiting her arrival. Each second that passed by, I knew that my intentions were crushed. The vow that I had made was completely crushed and I knew that as soon as I saw my family, I was going to fail. Pastor Kimbrough talked to me about how to use wisdom concerning our marred marriage. After several minutes of our conversation, my wife arrived in the yard. Pastor Kimbrough and I were leaning on the opposite side of the hood of his jeep as she was pulling in the yard. My eyes were like a red beam beaming directly into the back seat of the vehicle where my two stepchildren were. Yet the closer she drove in the yard, the swifter my heart was beating and the sweatier my palms had gotten. My knees grew weak and thoughts raced through my mind like cars racing in a Daytona 500 speedway race in Talladega, Alabama.

The children got out of the vehicle first with excitement running to give me a huge hug saying, "Where have you been? We missed you so much. "Before I could attempt to answer their question, my wife popped the trunk of the vehicle and I noticed it full of groceries. I glanced at Pastor Kimbrough as he remained crutched on the hood of his jeep. He had this expression on his face that actually spoke to me saying, "Go ahead. This is your family. "I compassionately embraced my step-children with a hug and a smile. I can tell by the excitement that was in their faces that they were very glad to see me. I looked once again at Pastor Kimbrough with a deep look of the expression speaking, "What do I do next?" Amazingly, he answered my thought as if he was inside of my brain while my stepchildren were still abreast to me in my arms. He whispered very softly to me saying, "Son, go get those grocery bags for your wife. Look her directly into her eyes and say, "I'll get them for you."

It seemed like it took her forever to get out of the vehicle almost as if she dreaded to be near me. Finally, she got out and attempted to go to the trunk of the vehicle. I said, "I'll get them for you." She said, "Thanks! I really appreciate your assistance." Her voice touched my innermost parts so deeply and I felt myself being tremendously tempted to reconcile. When I completed the voluntary job of getting my wife's grocery bags out of the trunk of the vehicle, I went into the trailer to go to the bedroom to get my personal belongings. While I was packing my belongings, my stepchildren gripped me on my arms asking me, "Where are you going? You just got here and you're already leaving?"

They were standing in my presence with tears leaping from their eyes asking me repeatedly to please stay at home so that I could spend some time with them. I stood there also with tears in my eyes contemplating on how to explain to the children what I was doing and why. I stood there looking at them with great compassion in my eyes and in my heart, but leaving them with no answer at all. My wife also stood teary-eyed, yet remaining quiet as a mouse. I was so close to her that I felt her heart's cry. She didn't show it externally by word of mouth, but internally I saw that she was damaged.

Periodically, my wife and I would give eye contact to each other, and every time our eyes would lock, I saw a crushed and confused woman. I saw that she was crushed at the foolish decision that she made of detaching herself from me. When I looked at her again deeply, I saw her looking into the eyes of a changed man. Pride completely compassed her and she allowed her mind to say "NO" when her heart was screaming "YES."

When I finished packing my personal belongings, I headed out of the door to Pastor Kimbrough's jeep. Suddenly, I was gripped with the children's heart and tears as they were crying out for me not to leave. I could actually feel the burning compassion on the inside. I placed all of my personal belongings into Pastor Kimbrough's jeep and asked him for a few more minutes to talk to my stepchildren. He consented and I went back into the trailer to talk with them. I explained to them in the best way I could what was going on. I made it plain so they could understand me.

I found myself forgetting that Pastor Kimbrough was waiting for me in the yard; I was so caught up with dialoguing with my stepchildren. When I looked outside, he was gone. I was so overwhelmed at this. He actually left me there. I really didn't want to go over there in the first place and now all of a sudden, he leaves me there. I was now doing what I repeatedly rehearsed that I wasn't going to do. Pastor Kimbrough knew that I really didn't want to be here, and he leaves.

Approximately ten minutes after I realized he had left me he called her cell phone to speak to me. She gave me the phone and as I bluntly answered, "Hello!" He replied, "Demetrius are you mad at me?" I screamed, "What do you think?! You left me! Wouldn't you be if I left you in an environment that you didn't really want to be?" He explained to me his reason for leaving saying that he desired for me to mend my marriage. He said that he saw their desperate need for me and his ultimate reason of leaving was to leave us alone so we could come together and reconcile as a whole. After Pastor Kimbrough and I finished conversing, I talked to my family, expressed my feelings to them and apologized profusely for my shortcomings. I ended up spending the night exactly where I said that I would never be a part of anymore.

The Lord's mercy and grace protected me from being caught up because I was violating the rule of being in my authorized area. I was supposed to be at Pastor Kimbrough's residence, but I was at our residence. If my probation officer would have called and found out that I wasn't at my authorized area, she could have every right to have me incarcerated. I thank the Lord for His mercy. The next morning, Pastor Kimbrough arrived to pick me up. I left my wife's residence and journeyed around the surrounding cities in Marion

County to seek employment. I put in many applications in several of places. For some reason, no one would show any attention to my applications.

Well, unknowingly, the Lord had something better in store for me. A week later, I got a phone call from the manager of South Ridge Homes, which was a trailer plant in Hamilton, Alabama. He told me that he looked at my application and was interested. He also invited me to have an interview with him. I shared the information with Pastor Kimbrough and we began to praise the Lord for what he had done. Pastor Kimbrough took me to the interview and we were confident that the job was mine.

When I got there and as I was entering into the building, I was thanking the Lord for what he was doing and what He was going to do. The secretaries and other elite individuals were very generous towards me and spoke with wonderful spirits as they escorted me to the plant manager's office. I was very anxious to see what God was going to do. After an hour of being interviewed, the plant manager said, "YOU'RE HIRED! WE'LL SEE YOU TOMORROW MR. GUYTON." I replied very professionally, "Thanks a lot! I'll be here on time and ready to work."

Internally, my spirit was leaping, but I kept it cool externally. You know that I had to act like I was used to something. Sometimes, we have to act as if we have some home training, yet in this situation, I was ready to jump through the ceiling. That day was so awesome, because I recognized the essence and the presence of God. He did it for me! When I got back to the vehicle to see Pastor Kimbrough asleep with great streaks of sweat dropping from his face, I awakened him with a holler saying, "I got it! The Lord gave it to me!" He was very elated for me and humorously stated, "You better have gotten the job as long as I was out here in this hot sun".

We left the premises and traveled to Pastor Kimbrough's restaurant, *O' Taste and See Soul food.* The restaurant was an establishment developed by the Greater New Beginning Baptist Church. When we made it to the restaurant, we ate dinner with many of the church members who also celebrated what the Lord had done for me. They were more ignited than I was about the Lord's blessing. After eating, communing, and celebrating, Pastor Kimbrough and I left the beautiful luncheon. As we were riding, he elaborated on my question that I asked him earlier in our relationship, "What is a man?" He said, "Son, now you're walking in the footsteps of a man". He also explained to me how the enemy was going to put his foot out to try to trip me up and destroy what the Lord had done for me.

He'd always pray over my life because he saw the hand of God in my life and he didn't want me to allow the enemy to slip in to take root in my life. I was still unlearned of what I needed to be on the lookout for. All I knew was that the devil was the bad guy and the Lord was the good guy, but what else? Was that it? The next day, I went to work with full enthusiasm and determination in my heart to hold on to this job. Pastor Kimbrough was my "taxi". He would take me to work and picked me back up.

I arrived on my first day earlier than expected so I remained in the lobby area until the supervisor or the plant manager arrived. During the wait, I began to praise, worship and give thanks to the Lord. I felt His warm love wrapping around me. I could hear Him whispering in my ear, "Son, I love you so much. You are so much of a value to me". I was in the midst of a wonderful worship experience and suddenly, the plant manager swung open the double doors. He shook my hand and said, "Mr. Guyton, I see you were having a personal time. I replied, "You wouldn't understand it if I told you. "As we went into his office, I was very amazed at this because I felt like a businessman. A real businessman!

I said to myself as I dialogued with the manager, "Here I am, a labeled and notorious thug in the office with a guy that has a suitcase doing business." This blew my mind! Next, I went through the orientation, watched safely movies, signed papers, and took a physical. He went over the pay rate salary with me and when he showed me what I was going to be making, my bottom lip fell to my toes. I almost fell out when he shared the pay with me. It was unbelievable! I knew that this was the sovereignty of God because I didn't have a high school diploma, a G.E.D., or any of the other requirements that they required, only Jesus. God stepped on top of the requirements and pushed the law out of the way just to bless me.

I was starting out with $11.45 per hour building ceilings for trailers. God had given me awesome favor with the supervisors. I didn't know how to perform this duty, but my supervisor assisted me. I knew that my facial appearance would have many curious, so I used it to my advantage for the glory of God. Many people began to see the power of God in my life. Many would ask me what happened, but they overlooked the scars and would say, "Demetrius, God has been so awesome to you and is still being good to you.

If no one can see the Lord's goodness in your life, then they just don't want to see it at all.

During all this, the enemy was so camouflaged that I couldn't recognize him at all. A few of my wife's family members were employed there also and they saw the favor of the Lord in my life. This was all one huge shock once she found out because I didn't inform her of anything that I had done. When I got off from work that day, I shared with Pastor Kimbrough and the family the favor that God had given me with my co-workers and supervisors. We rejoiced and praised the Lord for what he had done and what he was doing.

That same night, I heard a voice hollering from the backroom, "Demetrius pick up the phone! "I answered wondering who this could be at this time of night. When I said hello, I noticed that this caller was my wife. She angrily said, "Oh, you think that you're all of that now, huh?" Her tone was very disturbing and the spirit that she possessed was very unpredictable. I found myself compromising instead of letting my light shine. She continued to say, "I heard that you have a good job and that everyone loves you. Is that why you didn't want to come back home with me and my children?" She seemed more jealous than happy for me. Her response to my decisions to do and live better was to force her way back into my life. I tried repeatedly to mend my marriage, but she only rejected my request. Therefore, I knew that this wasn't a genuine greeting from her. So, I shook the dust off my feet and moved on.

I explained the exact same thing to her, but she wasn't receptive to this at all. After I cut the conversation short, she called back instantly stating that I was going to wish that I'd never met her and that I was going to wish I was dead if I wasn't already dead when she got through with me.

This was very, very crucial to me and I took it serious. I didn't know what to do concerning this and I didn't want to confide with Pastor Kimbrough about this either because I didn't want him to know what was going on. I thought that I could do something about this, but I found out different. I had a deep discussion with my heart and my mind. My heart calmly commented, "Do you still love her?" Furthermore, my mind whispered, "Should I stay or should I go?" No doubt, I still loved my family, but I refused to go back to the vomit that I had thrown up. So being solo was my decision and I supported it greatly.

When I began to support my own decision, all hell broke loose. It got so bad that her family had gotten involved. It was like I was against the world. I desired to leave and go to a place where I was unknown so that I could start my life all over again. It was easier said than done because Pastor Kimbrough's signature was on my release papers and that was my roadblock.

Mrs. Adine Kimbrough helped me enroll at the Bevill State Community College in Hamilton, Alabama where I attempted to get my G.E.D. I also was hired part-time at Burger King, which was directly across from the college. Everything was going great for me. Still, as much as I had been blessed, my wife continuously tried to destroy me by using what was dearest to me. She attempted the more to denude me. She would call and make statements such as, "You'll die before I allow you to be with another woman. If I can't be with you, no one else will." Yes, this sounds so crazy, but it's so true. The more I shook her and the family off, the deeper the ditch was being dug.

One day, I was at work, and Pastor Kimbrough arrived at my job informing me that the Hamilton City Police had come to his residence issuing a warrant for my arrest with the charge of harassment communication. I was crushed! I knew that this was a setup from hell that was designed to destroy me. I tried to justify the matter, but it didn't work at all. Pastor Kimbrough said, "Son, let me turn you in so we can get this over with. Don't worry, I'm with you." So I went to the police station and waited for an officer with my warrant in his hand. I screamed loudly, "What is this!" He said, "We have a warrant for your arrest for harassment communication signed by your wife.

They took me back to the Marion County Jail once again and gave me a $500.00 bond. This was such a miserable time for me because once again, I'm at the county jail for a false accusation. A revolving door is what I was going through because I just didn't clearly know how to utilize my weapons of warfare. This was a great set up to have my life destroyed. Please believe me when I tell you this, she was doing a spectacular job.

Have you ever been destroyed for doing the right thing at least the best you knew how to do? There was nothing that I could tell the guys at the county jail. All they could see was that Demetrius Guyton was back again. I only stayed over the weekend and Pastor Kimbrough posted my bond. During my stay, I lost my job at South Ridge Homes, but I still had my part-time job at Burger King and a chair in the classroom. I wanted to do away with my wife's negativity so bad that it was eating me up. I mean this was literally driving me crazy.

I called my probation officer and asked her for advice. She told me to make notations of every time my wife would trespass me, but my heart frowned at that. There was an unbelievable love in me that wouldn't let me do to her what she was doing to me. She also informed me to stay away from her as much as possible. Once she found out that I had been released and back on the streets, her hate for me increased.

One particular night, I was on the phone dialoguing with my grandmother and I got a beep. I clicked over to answer the other caller and amazingly it was my wife. She screamed to the top of her lungs, "I can't get rid of you!" She was calling me everything but a child of God. I knew then that it wasn't her, but the evil spirit that had taken residence inside of her. It was trying it's best to destroy my blessings and assassinate my identity.

I continued to live at Pastor Kimbrough's house and doors were opening very wide for me. God had given me favor with my probation officer. She allowed me to go anywhere I desired as long as I got it clear with her and was with Pastor Kimbrough. He and his wife took me to Mississippi to a church that he had to preach at and when we arrived there was a lady that stuck out to me. I noticed her staring at me very deeply and smiling. Every time I looked at her out of the corner of my eye, she was staring at me. This stare actually confused me because I couldn't comprehend this look at all.

After Pastor Kimbrough finished preaching, this same lady immediately arose from the pew and began to prophesy over me. It was amazing to me because what she was saying was so true and accurate. She began to interrupt the service and say to me, "God says that there's a lot that you do not understand. You've been crying all day and night trying to comprehend some things, but God says He hears your cries and He has your tears in His bottle. He also says that He desires for you to be in a place of contentment in seeking him. He loves you so much and He has a unique calling for your life. You're valuable to Him and you're His chosen vessel."

I was so befuddled, because this prophesy was too profound for me to receive. At the same time, this was a voice from Heaven because I had been continuously crying every night asking God "Why? What is it about me? Why is this going on in my life?" The prophetess confirmed everything that I needed answered. She would prophesy, sit down and jump back up repeatedly prophesying over my life. She would repeatedly say, "You're a chosen vessel! You are a chosen vessel! Let God get the glory through you! He wants to use you mightily."

As we were riding down the road, Pastor and Mrs. Kimbrough began to encourage me to stay strong. I received it and began to walk what the Lord had spoken to me in full manner. When I began to try to walk out what the Lord spoke over me, the enemy would rage greatly. For some reason, I couldn't resist the periodic cries of my stepchildren that occurred in my mind. So I found myself tip toeing back over to my old residence. I went to reconcile with my family and God knows I needed His strength.

For a split second, our marriage appeared to be promoting. We seemed to be so happy and acted as if nothing happened at all. We agreed to reconcile and restore our relationship as a family. I still was under the responsibility and authorization of Pastor Kimbrough because he was my co-signer. After I explained to her that I couldn't move as fast as she wanted me to, she transformed tremendously into a completely different individual. Instead of her being patient with me, she became very angry and I found myself debating once again. She wanted this to transpire quickly, but it couldn't be that way. She was unaware of my obligations of being on probation. Therefore, she grew angrier, because she thought that I was trying to use this as an excuse and dodge her. In all actuality, I was unknowingly flirting with Satan and slowly but surely, I was being set up for a great downfall.

I explained to Pastor Kimbrough what was going on, but he wanted me to continue to salvage my marriage. Nonetheless, the harder I tried, the worse it got. During the time I was supposed to be at work, I was secretly at my wife's residence. The more this went on, the deeper I was sinking into sand and getting choked out as if a boa constrictor had a grip on me. In short, I was a young man that was blind and in love. Recognizing and understanding what the enemy was doing was far from my imagination. The devil knew that and took great advantage of that weakness.

One day, I went over to my wife's trailer and stayed there all day long and half the night. While I was there, things appeared to be so unified. I loved my family dearly and I was willing to do whatever it took to see them happy, but I thank the Lord for thinking for me when I didn't even have a mind to think for myself. God foresaw something crazy that was about to occur and intervened on my behalf. We spent personal time together, talked about our life as a family and the importance of it. People would call her and she would postpone the conversation just to be with me. That sparked a fire when they found out that I was over there, they tried to tell her not to be around me, but she resisted their request.

People didn't want our marriage to be refurbished. While I was there, I received some criticism from my wife's family and friends who had called to talk with her. It didn't matter to me because all I wanted was my family back. As I was leaving the premises, we agreed to mend our marriage to the maximum regardless of what people said. She gave me the impression that she would wait until my probation period was over so I could move with my family. My plan was to get my authorized residence transferred from Pastor Kimbrough's residence to my wife's residence where I once resided, but the plan was completely demolished and it went the opposite direction. I'm so thankful that it did because the Lord used this as a bridge to really manifest Himself to me in such a powerful and miraculous way.

Chapter 11
A Journey In The Jungle

I believe with all of my heart that the Lord allows us to go through some devastating phases in life that amazingly becomes a catalyst to usher us to a higher and greater dimension in Himself. The Lord orchestrates our struggles to shape, mold and prepare us to be the vessels He desires to dwell in and utilize for His glory. Nothing is a shock to God. It may creep up on us, but not God. He is not shocked at all. I still find it quite amazing and powerful how the Almighty One can take a problem and transform it to a pearl.

I have learned that trouble underlines the fact that God is up to a great work in our life. One thing I can say is that if you continue to flirt with sin and allow it to caress you, it will soon choke you with such a grip that only the Lord's hand of mercy could release you.

The saying, "warning comes before destruction" is so authentic. I met a lady at Pastor Kimbrough's house not long after I left my wife's trailer where I was trying to reconcile and restore my family. I call her my messenger angel. She gave me a warning of the destruction that was ahead of me. She was a faithful member of Greater New Beginning Baptist Church and a dedicated friend of the family.

I knew that this was "Heaven Sent" because she spoke directly to my mystified soul. We were outside Pastor Kimbrough's house in the patio when she began to tell me, "Demetrius, I know that you love your family dearly and you desire to have them in your arms, but please, don't go back over to your wife's residence because I see something very destructive happening to you if you do. The time that you spent over there today was supposed to be your death decree, but God spared you. Don't fall for the enemy's trap! It's a set-up from the pits of hell. Death is riding you Demetrius and the assigned area is your wife's residence. If you want to continue to live, don't go back over to her house. Please, listen to this word. This is your word. It's all on you."

This information hit me in the center of my heart as if someone threw a dart to hit the bull's eye. I believed my angel's message deeply, but I was still blind for some synthetic reason. I was walking around with my eyes wide shut. I wish I had taken heed of her warning but sadly, unbelievably, I unconsciously chose destruction.

The next morning, September 14th 2005, I ashamedly tip toed into the destruction of which I had been warned the day before. I was actually on my way to work and my mind whispered, "Demetrius, go to your wife's trailer they need you."

I tried repeatedly to discard those heavy thoughts, but the more I did, the heavier those words begin to drum in my mind. I could literally hear those words in my mind clearly saying, "Demetrius, you have some time. Before you go to work, stop over your wife's residence because their heart is crying out for you." These words reiterated themselves repeatedly in my mind.

So I went over there thinking that it was going to be a brief visit, but unknowingly, I drove myself into a seemingly endless pit. I had my house arrest box with me along with my burgundy Holy Bible that I had gotten from the minister at the detention center in Greensboro, Alabama when I was a kid. As I was creeping over to my wife's residence, my mind was racing with thoughts of what could actually happen to me and what I was getting myself into.

A number of times on my way there visions would appear in my mind of me and my angel dialoguing the night before. Even as I drove to my wife's trailer, I could hear the lady's voice whispering to me, "Demetrius please don't do it, leave now". Yet, my love for my family was so incredibly injected inside of me, that my vision was blurry. If you had placed a "caution" sign in front of me, I would have thought that it was a "go-ahead" sign.

When I arrived in the yard and as I was walking onto the porch, I felt such a heavy spirit fall upon me almost as if a supernatural force was actually pulling at me. One side of my mind whispered, "No son, turn around and go back home." The other side of my mind was screaming, "Go ahead Demetrius, it's all good". I felt something just wasn't right about this. The atmosphere was very weird and I desired greatly to vacate the premises. Nevertheless, for some strange reason, I chose to pursue onto the front porch.

I knocked on the glass screened door about four or five times making it known that I was there. All of a sudden, I heard my son shout, "Mama, Demetrius is out there. Can I let him in?" Surprisingly, she wouldn't let her son open the door for me, instead, she made him be quiet and go back into his room. My stepchildren and I had such a bond that they could sense my very presence. They had drawn to me like metal drawing to a magnet. Meanwhile, I was building up with frustration, confusion, and anger because I felt that my wife was playing an immature game with me and I recognized that.

So I knocked on the door once more, but there was no answer. I decided leave the premises. As I walked off the porch, I took another glance back at the living room window and there was my wife standing there looking at me through the window with tears running from her eyes. She stared at me with the deepest stare ever. As her tears drained down her eyes, my heart began to frown at seeing my wife in such a disturbing manner.

My compassion grew great and I fell weak for the tears. As calmly as I could asked her to let me in the trailer so I could dialogue with her and embrace my stepchildren, but she only stared at me with tears in her eyes without blinking at all. I found myself getting deeper into confusion. In short, instead of this getting better it only got worse.

While we were staring at each other in the eyes for such a deep moment, the enemy was running devious thoughts in my mind such as "Demetrius, there's another man inside of there. You've caught her red handed. She's guilty! That's why she doesn't want to open the door. That's also why she's crying." Out of all the harassment she'd bring my way and the other foolishness that I had to deal with, I couldn't believe this at all. She was so envious at the blessed life I was living that she earnestly tried to destroy me. So I was stuck between deep dilemmas, something I've never encountered before. I couldn't believe what was happening right before my eyes. I was being played by my wife like a board game.

She was looking directly into my eyes and making moves at the same time, but I couldn't see it. While I stood on the porch in confusion, I saw a head walking across the living room of my wife's trailer, this stuck out to me like a sore thumb. It was true! She did have another man in the trailer. I completely lost it! I tried to leave, but my pride wouldn't allow me to leave knowing now that another man was in the trailer with my wife. This was the only thing I could visualize. My mind went completely void and life didn't even matter anymore.

Most certainly, I was very overwhelmed and broken-hearted. I was completely consumed with this crazy event. I remained stuck in the yard as if I was glued and couldn't move at all. A vicious thought was bombarding my mind. I was devastated trying my best not to let this offend me, but did not have the wisdom to know how to tuck my tail and leave. This led me to do a stupid thing that led me into a journey in the jungle.

After a split second of deep thought, I decided to force my way into my wife's residence. Can I be candid without receiving any criticism? Have you ever gone completely outside of your character to express an emotion? Furthermore, I must say that amazingly, the Lord took my mess and established a message.

I grabbed a gigantic rock and went back to my wife's porch warning her with a loud cry, "You better open up this door or I'm coming in!" She remained in the living room window with tears continually leaping from her eyes at the same time staring at me so deep that I thought she didn't think I would come in aggressively. I looked at her deeply and said to myself, "How in the world could she do this to me… G-THANG! No one does anything like this to G-THANG and get away with it." This was what pride was telling me, but at that moment, I was really an abandoned and perplexed young man.

I've been through many traumatic trials, but none like this. I guess "G-THANG" was showed that he could be humbled. After a deep thought, "G-THANG!" decided to throw the rock through the living room window where my wife was standing. When I raised the rock up to throw into the window, she vanished. The rock went through the window shattering the glass everywhere. It shattered on the ground and onto the floor in the living room. I threw the rock so hard that my body weight fell into the window and I found myself log rolling on the living room floor in piles of glass.

When I came back to myself from being intoxicated with anger and frustration, I stood in much pain physically, emotionally, and mentally. I was bleeding profusely in my heart and on my arms. I was also soaking in blood mentally to see this actually manifesting before my eyes. It was true! She was right! I recalled her saying that I was going to wish I were dead if I wasn't already when she gets through with me. I can truly say I felt like dying.

My whole word was destroyed. I noticed my stepchildren in the hallway crying because I was drenched with blood. I was upset with myself to know not only did I fall weak for "Delilah", but also I allowed my stepchildren to see me as a complete idiot. My stepdaughter was in great fear, but my stepson was elated to see me in this beast mode. He was young and didn't understand. I was so embarrassed and ashamed that my stepchildren who once adored me actually saw me as another individual.

When I recognized this, I took an "it doesn't matter anymore" mentality. So I grabbed my wife and threw her to the wall and said all type of vulgar things to her. Suddenly as I was staring in the eyes of my wife in deep despair, I turned to notice that there was not another man in the trailer. The enemy had inserted into my mind that it was so and I fell for the advice and the comments that he offered me. I felt like an idiot for real at this point. I had been hoodwinked by the devil with an illusion.

Suddenly, my stepson screamed, "Demetrius, the police are outside!" I looked outside and saw them all drawn down with guns. I believed that they had ultimate intentions to get me in custody or kill me. They swarmed the trailer as if I was a mass murderer or a notorious bank robber.

In that moment, I saw reality sinking down inside of me. I saw glimpses of my angel in my mind with tears in her eyes and I could recall her voice speaking to me saying, "Demetrius please don't do this!" I rebelled against my angel's warning and I had to deal with the consequences. She pre-warned me that I was going to die here at my wife's trailer and here I was willing to fulfill her prophesy. I just knew within myself I was supposed to get killed at my wife's residence. I thought deeply on what my angel had previously spoken the night before.

I hollered madly across the living room from the screen door as I was watching the police officers preparing to attack me, "See! Look at what you made me do! I guess you wouldn't stop until something like this happened huh! Well, here it is! I'm about to die! I hope it was all worth it! I'm going to make them kill me, because I'm not going back to jail anymore! I'm tired of life anyway; this is a favor for me!"

I attempted to step out on the porch and run just to let the officer's gun me down in the yard. My stepson screamed, "Demetrius, No! Don't do it! Please! I love you and I'm never going to see you anymore if you do this!" Compassion gripped me and I stepped back into the trailer and closed the door. I saw my stepson and his sister standing in the hallway with tears in their eyes. I looked at my wife and noticed her with tears in her eyes.

I was so hurt, yet, I was still feeling as if I had to hold the reputation of "G-THANG". So I said to my stepson "I have never been a sucker, I've always been real with whatever I've done, so I'm going to go out real in front of you so you can always know and see for yourself that you I was real. I love you and your sister, so always remember that." Then, I stepped outside to show myself to the officers and demanded them to kill me. I shouted repeatedly, "Do it! Do it! Do it! I'M READY! DO ME A FAVOR! KILL ME! I'M NOT GOING BACK TO JAIL! SO YOU MIGHT AS WELL SHOOT ME DEAD!"

Curious onlookers were outside observing what was going on and they all tried to get me to surrender, but I rebelled. The officers shouted, "Mr. Guyton! Please don't make us do this! Don't make it worse than it already is! Come on down from the porch and surrender!" Seconds following the invitation to surrender, I ran back into the house where my wife and stepchildren were to get a steak knife to "do it" myself. Have you ever tasted food before you ate it? That's how close I came to "doing it" to myself that I could taste it literally, but suddenly, my stepson shouted again", Please! Don't do it!" My stepdaughter who had been very quiet with tears leaping from her eyes also shouted, "Please! Don't do it!"

I couldn't let them see me cry. So I dried my eyes and thought to myself, it's time to do it or die. So for the love that I had for the children, I was obedient and didn't "do it". I threw the knife on the floor, went into the refrigerator to grab a strawberry soda, and sat down in the recliner as if nothing was happening at all. After drinking half of the soda, I stared at my wife with the same stare I gave my grandmother the night I left to go back to Jasper, Alabama as if I'd never see her anymore, hugged the children very tightly, and kissed them on their jaw telling them "I love you! Be good."

The driving force of the love that I had for my stepchildren led me outside to surrender to the officers. When I stepped outside, one of the officers was approaching the porch to grab me and I unconsciously swung on him hitting him in the jaw dislocating it dramatically. Another officer ran to wrestle me down, but I got the best of him and threw him down on his collarbone leaving him severely injured. It seemed as if I completely turned into the "incredible hulk".

God's grace spoke to the bullets that were inside of those black glock nine millimeters guns and mercy whispered, "No! I can't allow you to come out of this barrel to shoot my son. He's chosen, therefore, he can't die until he fulfills his purpose that was predestined for him before the world was created." The bullets were obedient to the Word and had no choice but to have "peace and be still."

Even as all of this was going on, the Invisible was doing the "incredible". My peripheral vision caught another officer running to attack me and I quickly jumped him throwing him to the ground. Then, I began to kick him and punch him like he was my worst enemy. While I was doing this, I felt a kick in my ribs. I looked up to notice a female officer. When I made eye contact with her she immediately began to back up as if she saw something uncontrollably evil on the inside of me. I got up with my eyes bloodshot red and walked towards her while the other officers stood intimidated. She quickly pulled out her pistol and mace while shouting, "Please don't make me do it!"

As incredible and unimaginable as these sounds, this is a true story. This is no fairy tale or a made up story. This is true. I felt led to tell you this because as you read, you might say to yourself "he's over exaggerating". When I look back, it's amazing to me also, but it's real. It was only by God's grace and mercy that I'm still here. At any given time, those officers could have shot and killed me, but the sovereignty of God held the bullets in the gun and the mace in its container, even when they attempted to shoot me.

Jesus had the power to say "PEACE BE STILL" to the winds and waves and they obeyed Him and He still holds the power to say, "DEATH, GET BACK AND BEHAVE, and it obeys. On that crazy day, death obeyed!

Jesus cares about you and me deeply. When I say deeply, that's exactly what I mean. It's beyond our understanding and comprehension why He loves us the way He does, but let me say, HE LOVES YOU DEARLY.

When the female officer shouted, "Don't make me do it!" I replied loudly, "What's taking you so long to do it! You'd better do it if you know what's good for you!" My wife screamed from the front doorway, "Please! Demetrius don't do this!" Then I told her, "I got nothing to lose, so I choose to do this, besides this is who you made me! I loved you, but now it doesn't matter anymore!"

The officers were determined to take me down, but I had already made up my mind that I wasn't going back to jail anymore. I was going to make them do their job. The other officers rushed at me with the threat of killing me for what I previously did to the three officers. I strongly resisted them and made my way back into the trailer to hide. I went to the bedroom and sandwiched myself between the two mattresses that were on my wife's bed. Yes, this is the same bed we use to lay on.

Suddenly, I heard an army stomping through the trailer like rams destined to grasp me in their custody. I silently screamed, "Lord, Please have mercy on me! They're really going to kill me!" As the officers bombarded the bedroom, I attempted to jump out of the window but I noticed that there were more officers on their knees surrounding all the windows. I was in a severe snare. In my mind, I said, 'It's over! There's no way out of this!" Finally, I lifted my hands to allow them to arrest and when I did so an officer struck me in my mouth with a club completely splitting my bottom lip wide open and knocking three of my teeth out.

The officers continued to brutalize me. They sprayed me in my eyes and facial area with some extremely hot pepper spray and slapped me continuously. I was hit in my head relentlessly with their clubs.

Be careful what you ask for because you just might receive it. I was asking for death, but the route I had to take to get there was unbearable. At first, it didn't matter, but that changed as I was enduring that beating from the officers in the kitchen of my wife's trailer.

My wife was quite terrified to witness the officers beating me so brutally. The children stood in the hallway stuck in amazement. The officers made them go outside with their mother as my stepchildren screamed to the top of their lungs to the officers, "Please! Stop beating him! You're going to kill him!" The officers ignored their cries and continued to beat me.

I could only protect my face hoping that they wouldn't destroy it any more than it already was. That left the remainder of my body vulnerable and the officers took advantage of it and beat me senseless. I was blind from the pepper spray they had sprayed in my eyes. After they got tired, they handcuffed me, hit me in the head two or three more times, and sprayed me in the eyes with the pepper spray once more. This beating broke me down. I had no strength, courage, character, or charisma. I was stripped of my all.

I know that my beating can in no wise compare to the brutalization of Jesus Christ our Lord and Savior, but I can sympathize with him greatly. This was a mild taste of the pain he endured for us. Yes, I said for us. It was so incomprehensible!

While the officers escorted me to the vehicle, I knew that this was the end of my life. I always knew that all I had to do was believe in my heart and confess with my mouth that Jesus is Lord and was raised from the dead, and I would be saved. I just needed some time to verbally recite it.

In the seemingly last few seconds of my life, I used the last few heartbeats that I thought I had to sluggishly whisper with blood everywhere, "Lord, I believe and I'm confessing that Jesus is Lord, Please save me!" I grew numb and unconscious to the world. I could still hear every word that was being said, but I was in a completely different dimension. I heard repeated shouts from my wife and stepchildren screaming, "He's dead! He's dead! You've killed my husband! You've killed my step daddy!"

Periodically, I felt touches that felt so much like the touch of my stepchildren. Internally, I was screaming, "I love you too!" This all happened in a flash. After being escorted and having to baby step to the officer's vehicle chained as if I was the most notorious person in the world, they opened the back door and threw me on the backseat. I laid on my stomach in the backseat of the officer's vehicle blind from the pepper spray that they had sprayed into my eyes.

My vision was completely gone. I wiggled like a worm to get in a comfortable position so I could sit up properly in the vehicle. The pepper spray was beginning to burn my eyes and my body so bad that I began to scream, shout and demand assistance from anyone. I needed help desperately. I banged my knotted head against the glass of the officer's vehicle demanding the driver to take me to a place of recovery. He only cussed me out and screamed, "Shut up before I spray you again! You're lucky if I don't take you to a back wooded area and blow your brains out!"

I shouted in reply, "Do it! Do it! How come you hadn't done it yet?" Seconds after my statement, I felt the vehicle stop, the glass window that divided the police and I was opened, then, the officer sprayed me again in my face and closed the glass window back. My whole body was burning as if someone had poured gas on me and set me on fire. I was in the backseat of the police vehicle trapped in a tight area that was clouded with pepper spray.

I was on my way back to the Marion County Jail once again on my last limb. This time, I was physically, emotionally, mentally, socially, and spiritually scarred. The only thing that I was desperately requesting was death. My life looked like it was one huge animated cartoon. I felt like the coyote that continuously chased the roadrunner, but never was able to capture him. When it appeared that the coyote had his hands on the roadrunner, he would holler "Beep! Beep!" and flee leaving the coyote in a worse predicament than before. One thing I admire about the coyote, even though the roadrunner would run circles around him, he didn't allow that to stop or intimidate him. It only made him stronger, wiser, and better. He didn't give up!

As a kid, when I watched this cartoon I'd always wonder, "When will the coyote ever get tired of looking like a fool?" That's the ultimate comparison of this my life.

The Marion County Jail and I were very, very familiar with each other. I believe that the building itself, the parking lot and all the surrounding atmosphere began to communicate to each other saying, "That looks like that Demetrius guy that was here recently. I don't really know what it is about us, but since our first date, he's been a faithful returnee. He repeatedly says that he will never be back to see us, but somehow he keeps coming to see us." This place seemed as if it had some kind of jinx on.

For some reason, I couldn't stay away from this den. I was trying to figure out what was it that I forgot to get or learn the previous times I was incarcerated here or what was it about me that was so attracted to this place. Truthfully, I had to learn that this place of obscurity was really my place of opportunity. It was something there that I didn't fully grasp hold of and life was going to bring me back to learn this lesson to prepare me to fulfill my purpose and my destiny.

Have you ever had something or someone that wasn't attractive to you, but you were admirable and adorable to them, nevertheless, it looked like the more you'd reject them, the more they would gravitate to you? Then, when you tried to say "No" in a respectful manner, you had to change your character just to show them that "No" meant "No." Well in my case "No" meant "Yes" and "Yes" meant "No."

When I arrived at the county jail, I was so blinded by the pepper spray, bruised, cut, and knotted up that I just wanted a comfortable bed to rest. My vision was completely gone and I found myself like the blind men that desired for Jesus to give them their sight. I cried internally, "Lord, have mercy on me!" I also cried aloud to the officers, "Please, rinse this spray out of my eyes and off of my body!" The officers reply was, "Shut up you nigger! I'm not doing anything! I couldn't care less if you die right now! Sit there and die boy!" Then I heard someone say, "You're lucky that there wasn't a clean way to kill you. I want to blow your brains out!" The way I felt at that time, I would rather have been dead.

After a several minutes, I heard the double doors swing open and a voice yelled, "Oh my God! What have you done to him! Rinse him off! Rinse him off! He looks a mess!" The officers propped me upon what felt like a wall and began to rinse me off, but the way they leaned me up against the wall, I could tell it was forced with hatred and they were being sarcastic. The voice screamed again while they were rinsing me off, "Stop! I mean right now! Leave him alone! You're going to kill him! Give me the hose pipe and let me rinse him off before he dies!"

Amazingly, that same voice told me, "Mr. Guyton, be still! I'm going to rinse you off. Try to open your eyes so I can rinse them out also." I tried, but I couldn't. The pepper spray was so cleaved to my body it was like an ant on a hill of rice. The more water that was sprayed, the more intensified the burns and pain had gotten. The individual that was speaking to me noticed that I was helpless, so he decided to open my eyes and rinse them out himself. He repeatedly whispered to me "Mr. Guyton, this is going to hurt and burn, but I need you to be a man".

After the seemingly endless time rinsing my eyes, I tried to open my eyes, but I could barely see. Yet, it was a lot better than before. Astonishingly, the sun began to peak out from among the cloudy skies and it was as if God had sent me the brightness of the rays of the sun to open my eyes. The sun shone on me so brightly as I stood helpless against the wall that my eyes were immediately opened and it appeared as if I'd never been sprayed in my eyes. I literally felt the pepper spray running from my pupils like tears. I had gotten my sight back, but my skin was still irritated badly.

When I opened my eyes, I realized that I had a full vision. I saw that I was in the middle of the patio at the Marion County Jail with other individuals staring at me. I looked down at myself and I saw that I was the bloodiest person you could ever see. The best horror movie that you ever saw had no comparison to this bloody sight. I was completely drenched as if I had been soaked in a barrel of blood.

I had on a white T-shirt along with a pair of Enyce jeans and a pair of white Nike Air Force shoes. My attire was ripped into pieces and my white Nike air force ones were stained red. I hadn't seen my facial area yet, but I could pretty much imagine what it was like. I heard the same voice that rescued me speaking to me, but he was behind me. I turned around to notice that this was a jailor that took great interest in me the previous times I was at the county jail.

While I was standing outside looking at those faces and trying to rewind back the hands of time in my mind, the jailor asked me to turn around so he could get those handcuffs off me. I did as requested and he took them off one by one while at the same time searching my pockets. He confiscated my cell phone, Chap Stick, and my wallet that had $72.00 along with other personal information. Following this, I was escorted to a detox room, which was only a room the size of an elevator with a coffee table along with an eight-foot concrete slab for me to lie on.

The toilet was in this room was so unreal. It was a small squared hole that was made in the floor. It appeared to be approximately three inches wide and high with four metal bars in between them. There was no way possible you could use this bathroom especially if you had to let out what you had digested. It was so pitiful! I observed this room and I thought to myself, "Oh my God! What have I gotten myself into?"

After about an hour or so of doing a past inventory of my present situation, the jailor came into the detox room where I was to take photos of my brutalization that I endured from the officers. Then he took me into the booking room to get me to sign some paperwork. The instant I approached the room, the secretary was sitting there with such a disappointed look upon

pg. 100

her face. She was so disturbed at my return. When she saw me, she screamed, "Oh my God! Demetrius, what happened to you? It was that girl wasn't it? You allowed her to trick you, didn't you?" I remained speechless at the same time in terrible pain from head to toe.

She informed me, "Demetrius, I'm not angry with you. Something great is going to happen beyond this. Stay strong and keep your head up." After signing the paperwork and conversing with the secretary, the jailor took me back into the solitary confinement room. On the way back into this unreal room, I asked him, "Why am I going to be put in this area?" He informed me that he was told by the other officers that I was under the influence of drugs and alcohol, but little did they know it wasn't the drugs and alcohol that had me intoxicated, it was love.

I can unashamedly say I was young and unlearned. There was no justifying my actions at all. It still didn't change the fact that I was in jail and on my way to prison. So I went into this cold dark room and laid on the concrete slab. I stared at the walls and was very determined to know if the Lord was with me or not. Here I am in a solitary confined room lying on a concrete block about as long as a couch and wide as a coffee table with no pillow, no covers, and no direction. Yet, through it all, something deep down inside of me wouldn't allow me to give up. I believed that God had something in store for me.

I was stripped of my clothes, integrity, dignity, character, and attitude. The air conditioner was turned up to the maximum and I laid there in that freeze box. The officers would watch through an opening until they saw symptoms of freezing to death, then they would give a warning and guards would rush in to take me out and make me warm. When I was finally warm, I'd immediately be put back into the room to freeze in my boxers over and over again. Thawing out then freezing to within just one, two or maybe three minutes of death, then being thawed out again. This continued endlessly.

There was no way I could sleep at all. I looked down on the floor to see a hole with four bars between them defined as a toilet. The flusher was on the outside and the jailer came periodically to flush it, mainly when he felt like it. The pain of my body was so intensified and my back was against the wall of abandonment. I was crushed and I felt so alone. I couldn't even see myself in a mirror to examine my appearance because there was no mirror in sight. All I could do was to define my appearance according to my feelings and emotions. I was in a miserable and horrible state.

Whenever I would lie down on the concrete couch, the knots on my head would hurt painfully. There was no way out and I found myself being like Jonah in the belly of the fish. The Lord allowed Jonah to go inside of the fish's belly so he could realize the reality of his purpose. During the time I was in the "belly", I cried out to the Lord and I was confident that He heard me. Suddenly, a warm, sweet, and peaceful spirit hovered me so heavily and uniquely that I was assured that the invisible and intangible arms of God had incredibly embraced me. I could feel no more pain and I found myself numb being able to fall asleep on the "concrete couch".

The next morning when I awoke, I noticed a pillow under my head, cover wrapped around me, a plate of food and a glass of tea on the floor awaiting me. As I was eating my food, I heard a voice in my ears very tender and gently saying, "I love you son. You are my chosen vessel. I'm going to resurrect you from the belly of death to the bed of life for my glory. Through your testimony, many souls will be saved." I heard that voice so clear as if you and I were sitting beside each other dialoging. Yes, it was that plain. I silently replied, "Lord, is that you speaking to me?" Suddenly, the jailor opened the door and said, "Mr. Guyton, it's time for you to go to the population, Let's Go!" I looked in the light that hung in the ceiling of the room, smiled, and silently said "Thank you Lord. That was you."

Finally, he took me in the dressing room and issued me a Marion County Jail uniform. At that moment, even though my clothes had been mutilated, I was so glad to have on a pair of clothes. Old man Willie was still there and he was grieved at my return. We dialogued very briefly, and then the jailor escorted me to the population where the other inmates were. They were on the edge to see me as if I was some governor, president, CEO, or an elite individual. I guess in their eyes, I was a criminal celebrity.

As we were walking down the hallway, the jailor asked me, "Mr. Guyton, how do you feel?" I replied, with a smile, and said, "I'm just fine sir." Before entering into the den with the other inmates, he encouraged me saying, "Demetrius, you stay strong. Keep your head up. You're going to make it." I agreed and appreciated him for the advice, and went into the den. When I heard the door slam, I was very persuaded at what the invisible had whispered in my ears.

This was the time where I began to seek for my purpose. It appeared to be cloudy at first, but as time went by "The Son" began to peak from behind the clouds. Of course, once again the guys were curious of my return. I explained it to them and they understood it clearly. Amazingly, I had an awesome peace over me and I felt very comfortable. It didn't matter anymore what had previously occurred at my wife's residence, which was the place we once shared together. The Almighty One had assured me that He was there and I was confident.

I knew within myself that the Lord had His hand in my life because I dog paddled out of a ditch of death in a delightful way. Others that went through what I've been through would have probably died, but for some supernatural reason God spared me. I made it! I can truly say, "I'M STILL HERE! KEPT BY MERCY AND GRACE." I didn't have a cell to go in because it was so packed, therefore, I had to ask the same individual that informed Mr. Franks of my return on the previous trip, or was it the one before that? Yeah, the same one I wanted to strangle for telling the preacher that I was in the cell hiding, I had to ask him could I share a cell with him. He along with his brother and his uncle were still there because they were incarcerated with the charge of capital murder.

They witnessed me leave and return many times. After the brief moment of trying to figure out where I would lay my head, one of the inmates shouted, "Demetrius, you look a complete mess! Your head is knotted up and bruised badly. You're scarred up severely and some of your teeth are gone!" The scars were there, but the pain was gone. I went into the cell to look into the mirror and I notice that I was damaged, but not destroyed. My head was knotted, up my bottom lip was split open, three of my teeth were knocked out, and my left arm was cut up tremendously, but there was no pain at all.

I couldn't stand to see myself looking that way. I had received thirty-nine stitches in my bottom lip. The external healing took three days. On the Sunday visitation day, I received a visit from Pastor Kimbrough and Adine Kimbrough. They were so perplexed at what occurred on September 14th, 2005. On the other hand, we had an awesome visit and they weren't angry with me at all. They were still willing to be my mother and father and my grandmother was still willing to be in my life unconditionally. They told me to stand on 1ˢᵗ Thessalonians 5:18, because this was the will of God concerning me.

The following Monday, September 19th, 2005, I went to court and got denied once again on my three year probation period and I was also awaiting another court date for my previous cases. The next day after I was denied, I was transported to divorce court and my divorce was finalized. I was so devastated at this denuding dilemma. But it was all good, I'd already possessed the revelation that the old me was ejected and the new me was inserted.

God allowed my church family to remain in my life. They began to show great love, support, and concern through it all like never before. That's what kept me strong knowing that through all my mistakes, failures, flaws, and imperfections, somebody still loved me. They promised that they would never desert me. They exhibited to me a genuine example of how a real family prays together and stays together. They took me in as their son, and I adored them as my parents.

Psalms 27:10 states, when my father and mother forsake me, then the Lord will take me up. HE DID IT! Mr. Franks was still faithful at coming to the jail to minister. I was so anxious to see him because I desired to share with him what I was impressed to believe. I wasn't worried about what he'd say or think about my repetitive incarcerations. On church call, he came into the block, and immediately came towards me with a huge smile, shook my hand, and asked me how I was doing. I replied, "I'm doing just fine Mr. Franks". He said, "Demetrius, you out of all people have something say." I just simply smiled and appreciated the Lord for His confirmation.

We had an awesome service in that den. During the service, I was commissioned in my heart to begin to facilitate a prayer group in the dayroom of the dorm every night at 9:30 p.m. before they locked down the cells at 10:00 p.m. I made signs saying, "Prayer Call at 9:30 p.m. nightly. WHERE THERE'S MUCH PRAYER; THERE'S MUCH POWER. WHERE THERE'S LITTLE PRAYER, THERE'S LITTLE POWER. WHERE THERE'S NO PRAYER, THERE'S NO POWER. I was obedient with that and I saw God move powerfully and miraculously through the prayers that we sent up. About 60% of the inmates were involved and adjoined themselves with me in this vision. Word spread throughout the entire county jail that I was doing prayer call every night at 9:30 p.m. and more individuals would gravitate to it. God really utilized the prayer call in that lion's den. I was able to persuade a lot of the ruffians and rebellers to join also. I explained to them the power of prayer and how God would manifest Himself through our prayers. It blossomed greatly and people began to believe God for outstanding opportunities and He'd move.

I began to be diligent and sincere in the things of the Lord. There were three women who faithfully attended the Sunday's visitation and just walk around the fence to witness to us about the Lord. They would always walk around the fence with their Bibles in their hands preaching saying, "Jesus is your only hope! Jesus is all we have! Trust Him! He loves you dearly!" Pastor Kimbrough and Adine Kimbrough would always be faithful at visiting me also. When I'd go out to the visitation yard, they'd always encourage me in the Lord.

One particular day, those three women paused their preaching just to pray God's blessings over my life. I was injected with so much confidence. They repeatedly reiterated to me, "Baby, trust Jesus in this. He's in control. He has great things for you." I agreed with a smile simply because God was slapping me in my face with His confirmation. After the visit, I went into the dorm informing the other guys to trust Jesus. He'll make "it" alright. The prayer group expanded greatly and the Lord continued to be the Sovereign One.

I remained in the county jail from September 14th, 2005 until November 12th, 2005 without knowing what I was charged with at all. My family and Pastor Kimbrough were also uninformed of my charges because the administration wouldn't release my information. So I asked the jailer of my charges and when would I be going to court. He informed me that I was charged with four counts of assault second degree; (three on the police and one on my ex-wife) domestic violence, burglary third degree, resisting arrest (multiple counts) disorderly conduct, criminal mischief, failure to comply, verbal assault, and destruction of property.

They tagged me with the label "a threat to society" and were greatly determined to hide me for a long, long time. My first court appearance was on January 9th, 2006. This was a day set aside to appoint me a lawyer. I was shackled from wrist to waist, from waist to ankles, leaving me only able to take baby steps. The courtroom was packed and I was very embarrassed to have the audience see me in that way. The officers made sure that I would appear to be the man that they broadcasted me to be. I was considered and advertised as an outcast, a nothing or a nobody. Some told me verbally that I'll never be anything. Nevertheless, God saw things different!

I'm so glad that God doesn't chose individuals that way man does. We choose people that are a jewel in our eyes, but God chooses the raggedy jewelry box, because he knows and sees what's inside. This degrading moment in my life was when the Lord's proficiency reigned in my damaged, trashy world. He really manifested Himself to me. Therefore, I had no doubt that he was alive, awake, and in control.

While I was at court, I had an opportunity to sit and fellowship with Pastor Kimbrough. I felt more relaxed with him being there to support me. As we conversed, he encouraged me not to be intimidated by what my circumstances looked like, but only trust Jesus because God was going to get the glory through this. So I agreed with a sincere heart. Finally, the judge called me to his bench and began to criticize me for my perpetual trips of being incarcerated and in front of his courts.

We discussed my cases and he explained to me that I was faced with a life sentence in the Alabama Penal System. Within, I was screaming, "You've got to be crazy!" After the discussion of my cases and the appointing of my lawyer, I was still able to dialogue with Pastor Kimbrough about thirty more minutes. So we prayed and believed God for a supernatural miracle concerning this situation. He also reiterated his love and support to me saying sincerely, "Son, don't worry about anything. I'm with you." They finally cut us short and I had to go back got to the county jail.

When they were escorting me downstairs to the first floor, I saw many associates that I was familiar with. They encouraged me to continue to stay strong and that this was going to work out for the good. It's so amazing how constructive criticism and encouraging words can give you peace in the midst of a thunderous tsunami. I knew that something great had to be birthed from all of this pain and grief that I was wrestling with. Indeed the Lord was confirming that through people.

When we arrived back to the county jail, the guys were anxious to know what took place with me at court. They asked me repeatedly, "Demetrius, what did they do?" I told them that they did nothing but gave me an appointed lawyer. They replied, "Man! You're going to get slaughtered with only having a court appointed lawyer, especially with the cases you possess." They didn't know that I had "The Lawyer" on my side that the court couldn't. I remained strong in the Lord and stood firm on His word. I refused to allow their illusions and disbelief to hinder me from what I had on the inside: A PROMISE!

They kept me in custody for another month and a few weeks before I went back to court for my second appearance. On February 21st, 2006, I went to plead day. Plea day is designed for you to accept the time offered or decide to take it to trial hoping that you could accumulate enough evidence to win the case. I rejected the offer they gave me and was taken back to the county jail.

I called my grandmother periodically just to inform her that I was still breathing and maintaining strongly. I also wanted her to be calm, cool, and collected about this circumstance. Therefore, even in the roughest and toughest times, I would tell her that I was just fine. My court appointed attorney would come to the county jail to visit me occasionally. On one occasion, he told me, "Demetrius, the best I could do is a life sentence. You have a handful of felonies, and a handful of priors, and many misdemeanors. That's all I can do!" I rejected his offer.

Days later, he came back to visit me in an enthusiastically manner. He informed me that he was able to work a deal with the district attorney and the judge. The offer was sixty years. I screamed, "Are you crazy! That's not a deal! That's a disaster! I might as well embrace the life sentence! What's the difference?" After my rejection, a week later he came to visit me again. This time he happily said, "Mr. Guyton, I have a deal for you. I replied, "What's the deal?" He stated that the judge and the district attorney agreed to give me thirty years. I refused to accept that as well. I believed God for a dynamic move on my behalf.

I greatly appreciated him for his support and assistance but I fired him and decided to let "My Lawyer" be my lawyer. To the courts I was solo, but I know that God and I were a dynamic duo. After visits with my court appointed lawyer, those hideous and horrific offers led me to the wilderness to cry out to the Lord for a great move.

My final conversation with my court appointed lawyer was on March 6th, 2006, which was on a Monday. The following Thursday at church service, Mr. Franks prophesied that the Lord was going to show Himself strong in my life. The next day, March 8th, 2006, I was called by the judge to appear in court. This was a special day set aside just to bring my cases to a closure. There were no written documents stating that I'll be appearing for court. It was such a shock to everyone at the jail once the news spread abroad.

The proper protocol is to inform the inmate that he has a court appearance prior to the exact day, but it didn't happen that way. It was impromptu. I was lying on my back in my cell by myself, thinking to myself, "Lord, when will you show yourself strong." Suddenly, around 4:00 – 4:30 p.m., I was awakened by the jailor. He informed me that I was needed desperately at the courthouse. So I hurriedly put on my white county jail apparel, brushed my teeth, washed my face, and went to the hallway where two officers waited ready to shackle me.

Internally, I was questioning God, "What's this?" I was very nervous because I was unlearned of any of what was happening. Many times, God's way of blessing you can worry you at first before it brings you joy because you're like "What's this?" This was something remarkable that the Lord was doing because at this time, the courthouse was supposedly getting ready to close. As I baby stepped to the transporting van escorted by two officers and the sheriff, I whispered to my inner most, "Ok Lord, this is your doing. My life is in your hands. So, move according to your word sake."

Finally, I left with much confidence in my heart, even though I was shackled like a terrorist, I was as free as a bird. When the two officers and the sheriff brought me into the courtroom, I noticed Pastor Kimbrough sitting down on the pews with such a delighting smile on his face symbolizing great confidence that everything was going to be just fine. The courtroom procedure of the family and an inmate is that they sit on opposing sides, but the sheriff allowed me to be able to sit down beside Pastor Kimbrough. I saw the essence and felt the presence of the Lord all around the courtroom.

As I examined the courtroom thoroughly, I recognized that there was nobody in the courtroom, but Pastor Kimbrough the sheriff, the two jailors and myself. I supposed that the judge and the rest of the people were in the chamber getting ready. Pastor Kimbrough and I prayed in front of the officers and the sheriff while the judge was on his way out. He also located the text Matthew 10:19-20 and asked me to read it. He told me, "Son, don't worry about anything. Open your mouth and let God be God."

Finally, the judge came out with this disastrous countenance on his face as if he'd just lost everything he worked hard to accumulate. Along with the judge were the court reporter, and the district attorney. Altogether, it was I, Pastor Kimbrough, the judge, the district attorney, the sheriff, and the reporter. The other two jailors had to go back to the county jail to attend to the other inmates. Pastor Kimbrough reminded me once more to relax and to be comfortable. It was easier said than done, but somehow through the sweaty palms and racing heart, I gained courage to do so.

The judge called my name and asked me to approach the bench. When I arose from the pews to approach the judges' bench, I looked at Pastor Kimbrough with a deep stare as if I'd never see him again. He smiled and patted me on my side and said, "Go ahead, it's alright". Then, I took baby steps toward the judge's bench. I swore in and took the stand. When I attempted to sit down, I noticed that Pastor Kimbrough had left the courtroom.

Whoa! I really had to lean on the Lord. My confidence support and crutch was gone. My encouraged heart immediately went to the lowest degree ever. It was me against the world! Nevertheless, I began to truthfully testify about what occurred at my ex-wife's trailer on September 14th, 2005. The Holy Spirit showed up greatly and began to speak so profoundly through me. It blew my mind the way I spoke with such boldness and clarity. My life was on the line and my hand was in the lion's mouth therefore, I had to ease it out instead of jerk it out.

I found myself asking the judge to put himself in my shoes as I attempted to testify. I asked him, "What would you do if you saw another individual in the house with your wife?" After I boldly asked him that question, I saw the Lord really dealing with his heart (Proverbs 21:1). The judge immediately began to sympathize with my pain as if he had been a victim of this issue before. I realized that he had a job to perform, but I also recognized that he was a man just like me.

He'd put up his guard by using the three officer's hospital bills that I resisted from and assaulted. He showed me the bills and began to threaten me with the maximum time of servitude possible. Instead of a life sentence, 60 years, or 30 years, I was actually faced with 199 years. The Lord utilized the least expected one, the one who was designed to nail me to the cross, the district attorney. She began to tell the judge how people from society had stampeded to her office to speak constructively on my behalf. The witnesses that were looking out of their windows standing out of their trailers and homes to observe what had taken place were actually on my side.

They told the district attorney that they saw the officers beating on me in the yard that morning. This mystified the judge as well. The district attorney was actually speaking sincerely for me. The judge found out that the officers had brutalized me and had them called in to testify. The Lord softened the district attorney's heart so much so that I thought she was my lawyer. She was actually speaking and fighting on my behalf. It was incredibly amazing and unbelievable. The two male officers arrived to testify, but for some reason the female didn't. Thank God she didn't! As they began to testify against me, the judge interrupted their testimony and asked them, "What gave you guys a reason to jump on this young man? Many people witnessed this and are willing to stand for and with Mr. Guyton."

The sheriff gave the judge the photos that the jailer had taken previously of me being beaten by the officers. The judge and the district attorney pressed the issue so persistently that the officers grew angry and actually left the courtroom being full of guilt. The judge called for them to come back to the courtroom but they kept walking. In short, the judge utilized this to finalize my cases. He along with the district attorney agreed to discard the assault cases I had on the officers and the rest of the felonies I had accumulated. They also dropped the misdemeanors that I possessed as well.

Suddenly, he paused from the courtroom affair and questioned my appearance. God opened a door for me to testify about His goodness. The judge knew that I had been battling with anger and frustration all of my life, nonetheless, he humorously stated, "Mr. Guyton, you whipping on my officers wasn't a wise way of letting your anger out, but you done an awesome job of it".

Then, he began to speak sympathetically saying, "I'd be less than a man to give you all of this time in prison. I couldn't sleep at night. I have a child also and I'd appreciated someone to have mercy upon him if he found himself in a jam. What I am about to do is not for you, but for me." It began to be a very tearful and serious moment as he was dialoguing with me. Instead of us having court we were having a talk show.

It was far past closing time, yet we continued to hold the talk show, I mean court. He continued to say all you needed was someone to be there to motivate and encourage you. You're a great kid with great potential. Life has been hard for you and I can see it has. Mr. Guyton, I want you to become a man. The man I see inside of you. I don't know if he was a saved man or not, but I surely thank the Lord for him.

At the conclusion of the court, I was asked to plead guilty to the burglary third degree case that I possessed for throwing the rock in the window and was given a 10-year sentence with good time, meaning that I would only have to serve 40 months or three years and four months. The ten year sentence I was issued overrode my three year probation period that had been revoked. So I had to serve a ten-year sentence instead of three-year sentence.

I didn't understand the good time policy and how you would only have to serve 33% of your time. All I knew is that ten years sounded a lot better than the previous offers. Even though in my mind I was saying, "Man! I'd be 31 or 32 when I get out of prison." The district attorney informed me that I was going to be eligible for parole after serving only a year or two. She also told me that I had a possible lawsuit on the officers that wrongfully arrested me and had beaten me.

Before my departure of the courtroom, the judge encouraged me with some powerful knowledge. He said, "Mr. Guyton, you've been given many opportunities that others would do anything for. I've been merciful to you. Don't ever come back in front of me or I'll make an example of my anger out of you. "Yes sir. Thank you so much" I replied as I happily attempted to vacate the premises of the courtroom.

On my way out of the door, the district attorney asked the sheriff for a few minutes to dialogue with me alone. He consented. So I tiptoed into this room with the district attorney and she looked me in the eyes and said, "Mr. Guyton, don't be intimidated by prison. I know it is an uncomfortable environment and you would rather be at home, but there is a reason behind this. I want you to go down there and find it out." I agreed with a smile.

She continued speaking, "Mr. Guyton, it's something so special about you. I see a very prosperous man that was blinded and derailed by the effects of life. You've been dealt a hand that you must play and make the best out of it. I went to bat for you so your life wouldn't go down the drain. You

pg. 111

are special and unique. The rest of your life in prison wouldn't benefit you at all. You just need love. So, be who I see inside of you. You're the only person in my history of being a district attorney that I've actually spoken for and gave the best for which should've been the worst. Mr. Guyton, I see a very bright young man whose been driven away by the storms of childhood. I believe in you. You're going to be someone special in the eyes of the world. Just stay strong and don't look back. Be good."

I blushed bountifully at her awesome words of edification while also being drenched with my tears. I replied sincerely, "Yes Ma'am. Thank you so much." Finally, the sheriff escorted me downstairs to the transporting van. On our way back to the county jail, the sheriff made the comment, "Mr. Guyton, I've never seen this happened before in all of my time being here. They were very, very merciful to you. I answered with a never-ending smile also being filled with great joy on the inside.

This was the Lord's doing, it had nothing to do with the elite people. Although the people saw it as so, I saw it as a miracle and a blessing from God Himself. Unmerited favor! I didn't deserve this at all! I did deserve the lethal injection or life without the possibility of parole. But God who is rich in mercy... I praised the Lord within my soul all the way back to the county jail. This amazed the entire county and all that had heard about it once the news spread abroad.

When we arrived, the news was already there. I didn't know how so quickly, but amazingly it did. As I got out of the van, the trustees, cooks and other officers said, "Demetrius, we heard that you got blessed." I just smiled and kept on baby stepping into the building. I couldn't wait to go back into the population to inform the other guys of the power of God and prayer. The miraculous move that God maneuvered in the courtroom was genuine evidence that He was actually hearing our prayers.

When I approached the dorm, the guys said, "Demetrius, we heard about what happened today. You truly were blessed. I wished that I could've had an opportunity like you did. God is truly with you." I replied, "Men, prayer is the key." The signs and wonder flourished the prayer group like never before. They believed God and He continued to move powerfully. The guys couldn't wait until 9:30 p.m. for prayer group. If I was caught up for some reason and it was getting close to 9:30 pm, the guys would remind me, "Preacher, you know it's almost 9:30 p.m. right now, it's time for prayer".

I'd reply like always with a great smile of joy. The following Thursday night after court, I was called to be transported to prison. I was very intimidated to inform my fellow inmates of this news, because we had a strong relationship. We were a family. When they found out that it was my time to depart and go to prison, they wept and hugged me strongly saying, "Preacher, we're going to miss you. We wish you can stay with us or we could go with you but we understand."

It was a very touching moment and feelings really aroused from true brothers who had gained courage to follow Christ. I didn't depart until 5:00 a.m., so I had time to fellowship with them and pray with them before they called lights out and lock down. When they called me out, I had to get my mattress, blanket, sheets and other miscellaneous and bring them out into the hallway so they could confiscate them. I had to sleep in the dayroom on a mattress. We prayed collectively one last time at 9:30 p.m. and they asked me to lead. I prayed blessings over each and every one of their lives.

After 10:00 pm lockdown, the guys stayed up all night and fellowshipped with me. We had to dialogue under the door where there was about an inch gap between the floor and the bottom of the door. They laid on the floor and we went down memory lane. We laughed together and mourned together.

There was another strong brother that I met named Mr. Brandon Posey. This was one of the three lady's brother that was coming to the county jail on visitation days to minister. I passed the torch to him and asked him to keep the prayer circle going. He agreed. When my time came to leave, the guys gave me their farewells. The officers couldn't believe how much of an impact the Lord used me to have in the other inmates' lives. The jailor said, "Mr. Guyton, they really do love you don't they?" I smiled as usual.

Suddenly, the inmates, my friends hollered in concert, "We love you Demetrius, be good" from under the crevices of their cell door. I replied sincerely, "I love you guys too. Stay strong and keep your heads up high." Finally, the officer took me down the hallway and shackled me down like usual and escorted me to the transporting van. I was on my way to Kilby Correctional Facility.

Chapter 12
The Power Of Connection

When I got onto the Marion County transporting van, what was once a nightmare became a reality. It was actually real. I couldn't believe it before my very eyes. I was actually shackled and on my way to prison. It took me a long time to wake up from this nightmare. In short, what appeared to be the worst situation in my life actually turned out to be the best situation in my life. No! Don't get me wrong, I didn't want to go to prison because I had been suspended from society, my family, and loved ones. Nevertheless, God knew what was best for me and He used the Alabama Department of Corrections to open my eyes of understanding.

The entire three-hour trip from Hamilton, Alabama to Mount Meigs, Alabama where Kilby Correctional Facility is located, I was in deep meditation of what was before me. Fear grew greatly because I was facing the unknown. I began to persistently pray and ask the Lord to be with me like He was in the Marion County Jail and on other occasions. Afterwards, I felt a comfortable and peaceable sensation shadow me. Even though I was physically bound in shackles, I was spiritually free in liberty! I laid my head back on the arm of the seat and trusted the Lord.

Eventually, I fell asleep and had a powerful vision of seeing myself in the presence of thousands preaching, teaching, and sharing, my testimony of how I escaped death ONLY by the predestinated will of God. I saw nations of people being set free, saved and delivered. Suddenly, a tenor voice had awaken me screaming, "Wake up Mr. Guyton! We're here! Let's go! I looked around to notice that I was at the back gate of Kilby Correctional Facility.

When I got out of the van shackled as if I was a notorious flight risk, I looked into the bright sunny sky and I heard a VOICE saying, "This is the beginning of the new Demetrius Pierre Guyton. I've chosen you to myself." A smile began to appear in my heart and on my countenance. Moreover, I walked into the prison with great confidence that the Lord was with me.

As the officers were escorting me into the building people were yelling, "Meat, what are you doing in prison!" Just as I felt, these individuals that apparently knew me couldn't believe what they saw themselves. I couldn't actually see who was hollering my nickname because the barbed wire fences were set up in such a way that you couldn't see but only hear. Nevertheless, I became comforted to know that I had some familiar associates there. I went through the process of being admitting as an inmate officially. This was so unreal to me. We had to get nude in front of many hundreds of individuals, get finger printed, haircuts, mainly baldhead, get photographed while holding an Alabama Department of Correction identification board and we also got sprayed down with lice killer as if we were animals.

Finally, I changed from the Marion County Jail jumpsuit to an Alabama Department of Corrections uniform. I was officially a prisoner. Afterwards, I was assigned to go to the east dorm. This was a den with the capacity of four hundred men from all over the state of Alabama. Men that you see on the television charged and convicted for outstanding charges I was now connected to them twenty-four seven.

I met several men that I was very familiar with from my hometown, Jasper, Alabama. I also met other men from the different areas where I lived. They began to ask me, "Demetrius, how did you end up in prison? This isn't your environment at all. You don't belong here." I explained my situation to them and it became a testimony to the men and they were astonished and heart touched at the same time.

Shortly after the conversations I held with others, I felt a hand touch me on my right shoulder. I turned around and the individual said, "Hey, aren't you Demetrius?" I replied, "Yes, I am Demetrius. I paused, looked at him deeply, and asked him, "Who are you and how do you know me?" He stated, "My name is Antwan Murry, some call me Tony. I'm from Bessemer, Alabama. I'm your ex-wife's best friends' boyfriend. I've known her for years." I was very familiar with his girlfriend, but not with him. Nonetheless, our spirits adjoined and bloomed with great friendship.

Antwan grew into being a "brother" to me. He stated that he saw me in Winfield, Alabama with my family periodically when he was out with his girlfriend. Due to this guy being so familiar with my family, and me I got comfortable to be able to call him my friend and this connection fitted together like a jigsaw puzzle.

We stayed in east dorm together for almost three weeks. While we were there we opened up with each other as if we had known each other for years. He gave me great knowledge and understanding that he had gained from his trials that he once wrestled with. I was very attentive and receptive because I was at a stage of brokenness and I would look for God in the small things, even in the words Antwan shared with me. We agreed to tag team to minister to the other guys that were in the dorm with us. Most of them would receive us, but there was also a crowd that gave us devastating opposition. They called us fakes, phony, and jailhouse preachers that were only perpetrating.

They wouldn't receive us because we had on a white uniform just as they did. Their ultimate excuses were, "We don't want to hear anything you two have to say at all. You have on white just like we do! How can you tell me anything? We don't want to hear anything you guys have to say!" Consciously, they didn't realize that it wasn't us that they were rejecting, but the Lord. So we took the criticism with a smile and journeyed on to fulfill the mission that we felt compelled on the inside of us to do.

We also agreed to have a Bible Study together at Antwan's bed. Every night we would call, "Church Call" in the back area. This was to alert the "hungry and thirsty" that we desired to assist them in getting "filled with righteousness". We had faithful men to participate, but the rebellious crew was very active. As a matter of a fact, they tried earnestly to stop most of the men from coming to our study, but the Lord won that battle.

On March 27th, 2006, we were separated and assigned to different dorms. I went to G-dorm and Antwan went to M-dorm, which was directly behind G-dorm. Our fellowship was reduced because of that transition, but when we did see each other, we would continue to encourage and edify each other by saying, "Somehow, someway, we're going to make it to the other side".

On one particular night, Antwan and I had an opportunity to go to Kilby Correctional Facility's chapel called Peniel Chapel. The Lord really spoke to my soul on this night. There was a twenty-year-old inmate who was the speaker for the night. I'd never forget it. He preached a message titled, "How bad do you want it?" My friend believe me, I wanted the Lord bad. Not because I was in prison, but because I wanted to be a completely different individual. I also didn't want to go to hell.

When this individual opened his mouth and allowed the Lord to speak through him, it inspired and motivated me greatly. Antwan and I were sitting beside each other and I would tap him and say, "Man, I see myself being used by the Lord in that manner." Antwan replied, "Demetrius, I was just visualizing the same thing". I was so attentive to the message because it was such a conviction and I knew that the Lord was speaking to me. Before the service was over, I ran to the altar with tears leaping from my eyes screaming, "Thank you Lord for saving me from hell!" While I was on my knees, I accepted my calling and told the Lord, "Yes, I'll do your will. I will be who you want me to be. Take this little thing and multiply it for your glory. All I have I give to thee!" Then the minister prayed over me while I was on my knees. Shortly afterwards, we left the chapel and was on our way back to the dorm.

I pulled Antwan to the side and whispered to him, "I received my calling as an Evangelist. The Lord has changed my name from Demetrius "G-THANG" Guyton to Evangelist Demetrius P. Guyton." He appeared to be more appeased them I was. He was already a minister. He informed me that he embraced his calling at the Jefferson County Jail in Birmingham, Alabama.

The next day, we went to see our classification specialist for our assigned permanent facility. My specialist assigned me to go to Staton

Correctional Facility, which was a level (4) four security prison. Antwan's specialist assigned him to go to West Jefferson Correctional Facility, which was a level (9) nine maximum security prison. We didn't receive that information though. We got together, prayed, and believed the Lord to send Antwan to Staton Correctional Facility along with me.

The following day, I saw my psychologist, Mrs. Johnson, who surprisingly was a Sunday school teacher. She examined my criminal record and noticed that I had many felonies discarded. This astonished her greatly. She actually saw through my cases that the Lord's mighty favor was bestowed in my life and she began to minister and encourage me. She would also say repeatedly, "Mr. Guyton, you're a very blessed man. God is with you. This is unheard of. I just evaluated an individual that has a life sentence for one assault case and you had many of them discarded along with other cases. You're a chosen vessel. Go and let God show you his purpose in your life. I love you and I'll be praying for you."

On April 10th, 2006, I was transferred from Kilby Correctional Facility to Staton Correctional Facility, which was at Elmore, Alabama. I never had an opportunity to tell Antwan goodbye, but I continued to believe God for his transfer to Staton Correctional Facility along with me. I was aware that God's blessings were following me, so the transition didn't even matter at all. I was fully persuaded that it was something at Staton Correctional Facility for me and I was anxious to grasp it.

When I arrived, I was already familiar with a prison environment. As soon as I got off the van, I saw the enemy influencing the men greatly. Violence was in full effect, openly and unashamed homosexuality was intensified horribly, gangbanging, etc... I thought to myself, "This is unreal! I must awake from this nightmare!" I couldn't believe it at all. I was actually in the jungle where the strong survived and the weak died.

I prayed passionately for a change in that place, and I asked the Lord to bring about a revolution. Once the procedures were done, I was assigned and escorted to B-dorm. I was placed in the center of the darkest place I've ever been. I maintained and stayed strong. I also let the light that I possessed shine in that greatly dark place of undeveloped individuals.

A few days after my arrival, I was impressed to walk around the track to meditate and pray. As I walked around the walking trail, I saw guys from a distance sitting in chairs, jumping, shouting, and clapping their hands.

So I curiously went to see what was igniting these individuals. Finally, as I approached the huddle, I noticed a guy evangelizing. I got a chair sat down and began to be very attentive to the Word. We had an awesome service and I desired to be a part of that lovely and lively brotherhood.

When the guy closed the service, I approached him, shook his hand, and introduced myself to him. He introduced himself to me as Mr. Donnie Jones. Mr. Jones was from Eutaw, Alabama. Remember this city? This was the place where I met and resided with Pastor Michael Barton. Mr. Jones had been incarcerated for (18) eighteen years for murder. He had a period of (25) twenty-five years to serve, but this was a sincere soldier for the Lord. I met others and they asked me to continue to come to church and fellowship with them. So I did.

On the following Sunday service, I met and individual by the name of Apostle Bokassa Montgomery, who was from Anniston, Alabama. Apostle Montgomery was the minister for that day. He had been incarcerated for almost (8) eight years for murder. He had a life sentence to serve, but he was a fireball for the Lord. Apostle Montgomery possessed a very, very powerful testimony. He was entrapped in a near death experience at the Calhoun County Jail. He was in a gang related riot and got stabbed many times in the left side of his face and in his back. He used to be "school yard Crip", but gave it all up to serve Jesus.

This guy was very knowledgeable in the Word and lived it. After he ministered this day, we got together fellowshipped and walked around the track. Apostle Montgomery and I had grown a bond parallel to Paul and Timothy or Elijah and Elisha. He was facilitating a new convert's class in the Teague Chapel on Monday nights. The class was designed for people who had recently become saved and desired to grow in the Word of God. Even though I had been saved, I'd still go to the class and remained faithful. I fell in love with the class because I was learning so much about Jesus. He saw my zeal and faithfulness and asked me to be his spiritual son.

He was Paul and I was Timothy. Everything that the Lord would reveal to him, he'd reveal it to me. He also informed me, "Demetrius, you're God's chosen vessel. He loves you and desires to use you greatly." Inasmuch, I became very diligent in the Word and in church. Eventually, I saw myself growing tremendously. I always asked Apostle Montgomery questions about certain things concerning the Word. No matter what I would approach him about, he always had an answer.

Led by the Holy Spirit, he would go out on the basketball court to minister the Gospel persistently and I'd be his armor bearer. I remained faithful to our covenant and our bond grew greater. I signed up for G.E.D. class that was held in A-dorm. The first day I attended the class and as I was sitting in the dayroom area on my ten-minute break, I was in prayer that Antwan would be transferred to Staton Correctional Facility. When I lifted up my head and looked around the Lord had answered my prayer while I was praying.

Guess what! Antwan was as at the microwave heating up a cup of coffee. He saw me sitting on the bench and came towards me with a gigantic smile on his face. I stated astonishingly, "Man, He answered my prayer. I was just praying about this and look." Antwan and I got together and we began to bond like never before. He had been assigned to A-dorm, which was where the GED class was. It was also across from where I resided. We were relentless with going to church services, the weight pile, and other recreations.

Antwan also joined G.E.D. class with me. Later on, I introduced him to Apostle Montgomery, who was residing in the faith dorm, which was E-dorm. We all bonded together in the Lord. We watched each other grow physically and spiritually. You can truly say you know a person when you're with them day in and day out. We suffered together and reigned together. We laughed together, and we wept together. We mourned together and we rejoiced together. We lived together and dreamed together. We constantly praised the Lord together and edified each other.

We had big dreams of becoming successful after our struggle. We always spoke those things that were not as though they were. Pastor Kimbrough would always tell me, "Son, if you act like you want to be, then you'll soon be how you act". So I applied this word of wisdom to my life earnestly.

I was moved from B-dorm to E-dorm where Apostle Montgomery was and days later, Antwan moved in with me. I met some awesome men of God inside of that dorm. They had outstanding testimonies and a lot of time to serve, yet, they loved and trusted the Lord with their all. This motivated me greatly. The life they lived in the prison helped me to overcome my turbulent times.

Apostle Montgomery introduced me to a guy named Apostle Walter Woodruff who was from Birmingham, Alabama. Apostle Woodruff had been incarcerated for (3) three years at the time for drug trafficking. He was an ex-pimp, drug lord, and a gangster, but he allowed Jesus to eject that from his life and insert the love of God inside of him. Apostle Montgomery and Apostle Woodruff were both leaders of the Staton Correctional Facility Ministerial Board, of which I later became a part.

I also had the opportunity to meet a guy named Evangelist Harrison Parham who was from Atlanta, Georgia. He had been incarcerated for (8) eight years at the time in servitude of a (17) seventeen year period. He was a part of the Crip gang and found himself in a shootout at the age of twelve. He was shot in both of his knees and man said that he would no longer walk any more. But God said, "Not so!" Evangelist Parham was thirty-seven years old at the time I met him and very active in recreations. He could out run any individual you put up against him. He was the fastest running guy at Staton Correctional Facility.

This guy had a gift that the enemy tried to destroy. He loved the Lord with his all. Evangelist Parham was the facilitator of the yard ministry. We got to know each other and our friendship flourished. He was also a "big brother" to me. I could always go to him about any issue, and he'd always support me to the best of his ability. If I was ever in need and for some reason he couldn't assist me, he would actually get upset and try his best to meet my need.

There were also other elders that continuously encouraged me in the Lord. They would go up for a parole review and denied release for two to five years and still be on fire for the Lord. I'd be like, "Wow, they really do love the Lord." They were not serving Him for what he could do; they served him simply for who He was.

On one particular day, Antwan, Apostle Montgomery, and myself were walking on the compound, and we ran into an individual that I met very briefly at Kilby Correctional Facility named Rev. Dr. Kita S. Moss. Dr. Moss was from Dothan, Alabama and very powerful in the Lord. This young man was twenty-nine years old and very uniquely anointed. His statue was mind blowing and to see Jesus use him would literally blow your mind. Dr. Moss was a very small guy 5'5" 125 pounds with the appearance of a child. He was in servitude for (3) years at the time and had a (25) twenty-five year sentence to serve following a 3 year federal term.

He was a youth pastor at Pilgrim Rest Missionary Baptist Church, which was very renown and resided in Montgomery, Alabama. Dr. Moss was a psycho when it came to the Lord. He had such a passion to live for Christ. This guy was very dear to me and I looked at him as a big brother even though he was small in stature he was a lot older than I was. I gave him the nickname, "a small piece of leather, but well put together". He had been in servitude for (3) three years at the time I met him.

Dr. Moss had been a student at Alabama State University and received his degrees in communication and counseling. He also graduated seminary in Albany, Georgia. This individual has many reasons to be a "lunatic" for Jesus. God spared him on many occasions. He was stabbed severely and faced death in a horrific car crash, but God kept him. He was assigned to C-dorm, but later relocated to the faith dorm along with Apostle Montgomery, Antwan and myself. There we really got acquainted to each other.

Moss had been in ministry for six years and had been exposed to ministry in society. Unlike us, he had experienced ministry on the outside. He had been previously incarcerated under the servitude of a twenty year split three sentence, but the Lord sent angels into his cell at midnight. A great earthquake occurred in the penal system and he was miraculously delivered. After serving only (11) eleven months on this sentence, he was blessed tremendously to be released. This was the beginning of his ministry.

As we dialogued, we came to the knowledge of realizing that we all had similarities that were instruments to glorify our God greatly. We were very serious when it came to Jesus and His Gospel. We consented to attack the enemy's kingdom with boldness, authority, and determination to destroy him. I had to be clicked up with some real individuals when it came to defeating the devil.

After a period of time, Antwan, Evangelist Parham, Dr. Moss and I were blessed to be enrolled at J.F. Ingram State Technical College which was located Deatsville, Alabama. This was so overwhelming to me because I never in life dreamed that a guy like me would actually be in college, especially while in prison. It was beyond my wildest dreams. Therefore, I was compelled to take great advantage of this opportunity to propel into a greater and higher level of education.

I signed up to take the welding class, but I never finished it because five months later, I was transferred to Bullock Correctional Facility and Antwan was transferred to Louisiana State Prison. Dr. Moss chose to be in the barbering trade and Evangelist Parham desired to be an aide.

On the first day of my attendance, the Lord blew my marbles. I was inside of the college walking down the hallway, and suddenly I gained an instant thirst for water. As I was walking in search of a water fountain, I accidentally passed by it unknowingly. In front of me about ten feet away stood a short brown-skinned lady standing by her desk. I said to her, "Excuse me, do you know where the water fountain is?" She replied, "Its right behind you. If it had have been a snake, it would have bit you." I smiled and answered her at the same time saying, "Thank you so much", not knowing that I was being set up for a supernatural blessing.

When I finished drinking the water, I started to walk down the hallway to go out of the double doors and, I spoke to myself saying, "Man! I can't wait until I get out of prison." My voice echoed off the wall and it caught the lady's ear grabbing her attention. Surprisingly, I heard this lady say, "Young man, come here." I went back to see what she wanted and the Lord Himself paid a visit.

As we began to converse, she asked me out of curiosity, "What is your name? Where are you from? What happened to your face?" I answered her questions truthfully and astonishingly, she pulled me abreast to her and screamed to the loudest, "God is so good! God is so good! Oh my God! It's you! It's you! I've finally found you!" I relied, "What do you mean you've finally found me? Who are you?" She introduced herself to me as Mrs. Jackie Harrell. She was the student advisor at the college and had been an employee at the pardons and parole board in Montgomery, Alabama. She used to be the chairman's assistant.

Mrs. Harrell continued to comment that she was very familiar with my condition, my situation and me. She informed me that she had done a relentless research on the case of the horrific incident that I endured in 1984. She continued to inform me that she assisted my mother by speaking on her behalf at her seventh parole review. Continuing speaking, she said to me, "I was going through a lot of files one day and I discovered your mother's file and her case caught my eye. I was so curious that I had to research deeply just to find out what made your mother do this to you. So I took the case and did research and at the same time, I was following up on you as well. Supernaturally, by the grace of God, you're here in my presence."

She had tears of joy and compassion leaping from her eyes and her love for me grew deeply. She repeatedly said, "Demetrius, this is so amazing. God loves you. You're a very strong man and I admire you greatly." I was awestruck at God's awesomeness. It was all coming together in my eyes. She had information about my mother that I had been secretly searching for, for a very long time. God used Mrs. Jackie Harrell to drop all I had been looking for in my lap.

Mrs. Harrell told to me about postpartum depression, which was a depression that women usually wrestle with after childbirth. This gave me a deeper insight of how it brings mental and physical pain to women. It also exhibited to me that women go through a difficult time of recovery. I myself began to search deeply on what post-partum depression was as well so I could be versed in this matter. However, can I be candid, before I even came to prison, I had love and forgiveness for my mother.

Regardless of what happen, I realized that she did something for me that no one else could ever do. So when I gathered all of this information together, I really opened the door of my heart wide to my mother. There was still one thing that I lacked, and that was to be able to see her. I desired to embrace her, kiss her on her jaw, look into her eyes, and tell her how much I love her and what she means to me.

Mrs. Harrell and I grew a great "mother and son" relationship, but there was nothing and nobody like my biological mother. I was very intimidated to open myself to her and share my childhood struggles. I did know that Mrs. Harrell saw me before I could see her. She could imagine the trauma and the derision that I had to overcome as a child. She was so dear to me and drew to me as a mother truly does to her child. That day when I arrived back to the prison, I shared the testimony with the other Christian brothers. They were so shocked. Furthermore, they desired for me to share my testimony the same night at church service.

The exact same night, God slapped me in the face with another extraordinary blessing. There was a female officer in the cubical, and for some reason, my spirit kept whispering, "Share you testimony with her. She can add gas to the fire of you testimony." The more I pondered on this, the more I heard, "Its ok go ahead." So, I finally was obedient to the still small voice.

I approached her and said, "Excuse me, for some strange reason; I'm in a debate with myself to share something with you". She said, "Go ahead and talk to my while I listen." I told her that I had been searching for my mother and I wanted to know if she could assist me in locating her. She said, "Who is your mother?" I told her my mother's name and she said, "I know your mother well." She proceeded to say, "I use to work at Julia Tutwiler State Prison where she was in servitude. As a matter of fact, I worked there for eleven years on third shift."

She characterized my mother highly and gave me some profound information that I could put together with the dynamic information Mrs. Harrell had given me. With this information, I was able to create a mental picture of my mother. I had gotten her head and her upper body all the way down to the waist. All I needed was to gain information that would give me a full picture of who my mother could be, her personality, character, conduct, attitude, and her charisma.

The following Friday night, the Lord opened the floodgate of heaven and let it rain on me. Every time I think about the goodness of Jesus and all he's done for me, my soul… Oops! I'm sorry; this is supposed to a book, right? Not service! Anyways, please forgive me, back to the story. The following Friday night, Pastor Richard A. Bland and his wonderful wife, Mrs. Carolyn Bland, founders of the United Prison Ministries International had a huge celebration at Staton Correctional Facility's Teague Chapel. I was very exhausted and I didn't feel like going at all, but my friend Dr. Moss, insisted that i do. Finally, I gave in and went to the service.

I was in desperate need of a rhema word from the Lord, so I went in the spirit of expectancy, but the sum of the expectation I had was so extraordinary in my eyes. God set the stage in great decoration, placed the microphone in place, it was on me to perform. While I was at the celebration, a lady who had been at Julia Tutwiler State Prison three different times spoke on how the Lord revolutionized her life from being an addict for crack to being an addict for Christ.

When this lady shared her testimony, I said, "This is it! This is it! I'm sure that she's familiar with my mother. At least once out of those three trips, she intersected with my mother. "So after the service, I approached her and asked her did she know my mother. She replied, "Who is your mother?" I told her my mother's name and she screamed, "Oh my God are you serious? That's your mother?" I stated, "Yes Ma'am. I'm looking for her. Do you know her?" She said, "Your mother and I are best friends. This is so unreal. I do not believe this at all! That's your mother?

She continued to say, "This is why I was assigned to come here on tonight. I was so tired that I really didn't feel like coming, but I did and this is the results." I said, "Really! I was exhausted also and I didn't feel like coming as well. Spontaneously, she shouted, the enemy tried to blind us from this blessing, but he is a liar!" She pulled me to her and hugged me tightly while tears leaped from her eyes, and at the same time, she shouted, "Yes, I know your mother very well. It's so ironic! You couldn't imagine the days and nights your mother and I cried out to the Lord hoping to see you one day and here you are."

I was so stunned at this because it was similar to the occasion that I encountered with Mrs. Harrell at the college. She continued to state, "Yes, I know your mother. I was her bunkmate. She was on the bottom rack and I was on the top rack." It took everything inside of me to keep me from collapsing. To me, this was a dream. I couldn't believe it at all.

She began to introduce herself and told me that she was a native of Birmingham, Alabama. She relentlessly screamed and hollered, "Demetrius, you're still here! You're still here!" We were locked together so tightly as if we were long lost lovers. I began to see the power of God take complete control of our fellowship. In the midst of our fellowship, she began to give me information that fulfilled my desire to characterize my mother mentally.

I finally had an opportunity to vividly characterize my mother. I attached the information that Mrs. Harrell had given me and connected it with the officer's information. Finally, I was able to bring a complete mental description with the information that my mother's friend had given me about her and was able to visualize an imaginary body of my mother. I had a mental picture of what I thought she would look like and what type of lady she was. My mother's best friend's information was the lower body part that flourished a perfect picture of who she would be.

With my mental description of my mother, I was able to carry her everywhere I went as if she was in my pocket or as if she was really there physically. She was always by my side. I made sure of that! I made a mental covenant that we'd never separate from each other again. I saw her hugging me, smiling, and saying, "Demetrius, I love you so much. I'll never leave you anymore."

My mother's friend gave me her address and we began to correspond as much as possible. She also informed me of the information of the whereabouts of my mother. In short, she told me that she would inform my mother that she had seen me at Staton Correctional Facility and that I was still alive.

I asked her to contact my mother whenever she could and tell her that I love her dearly. I also told her to tell my mother that I had gotten tall and handsome. My mother's friend was so grateful to have actually seen me in person. The Lord had answered their prayers and mine also. The next week, with such a surprise, my grandmother, Mrs. Ruthie Dunlap sent me a letter with my biological mother's address and phone number on it. What a blessing!

That same night, I wrote my mother a genuinely heartfelt letter telling her that the past was exactly what it was; the past. I also informed her that I loved her and desired her to be a part of my life as my mother and not an ex-girlfriend that found out I cheated on her with her best friend. The letter I wrote was assigned and appointed from heaven. The Holy Spirit assisted me as I wrote and I was able to articulate it very well. I also took photos and sent them to her. I anxiously waited on a response and exactly a week later on September 13th, 2006, I got a reply from my biological mother.

At mail call, I heard the officer scream, "Demetrius Guyton, come to the front. You got mail!" I went to receive my mail and when I looked at the return address and noticed my mother's name, I jumped as if I had won a million dollars, shouted "Thank you Jesus" continuously and ran around the dorm full of joy with tears streaming down my eyes. I continuously screamed, "I got my mother back! I got my mother back!" All the other guys including the officer had thought I went crazy and lost my mind. Truthfully, I did, but not like they expected. It was only joy! I knew that they wouldn't understand anyways. It wasn't for them to understand.

My friend Antwan was the only one that I'd deeply confide in, so he was very familiar with what actually took place. He came to me and asked me, "Demetrius, did she respond to your letter?" I jumped into his arms and shouted enthusiastically with tears in my eyes, "Yes she did!" I was so elated and I hadn't even opened the letter yet. Just like tasting food before you eat it, I could actually taste the tender nourishment of her words before I even opened the letter. I had no idea what was written on the letter, but I did have a desperate sensation to receive whatever she said. I was just so happy to hear from her.

Finally, after countless minutes of celebrating, I opened the letter in the presence of Antwan, Apostle Montgomery, Evangelist Parham, and Dr. Moss. Inside of this crackerjack box was a surprise that would make a three-year-old child jubilant and smile from ear to ear. There was a very beautiful photo of my mother inside of the folded paper. The t-shirt that she had worn on the photo said, "CAUTION! PERSON INSIDE OF THIS SHIRT IS SUBJECT TO FITS OF PRAISES." It knocked my socks off to see that she loved the Lord. Furthermore, she was iterating the fact that she really loved me and missed me dearly. I found myself crying as if I had lost someone dear to me. In all actuality, I was taking my soul through the Laundromat.

Mother was trying to justify what happened in 1984, but none of that mattered to me at all. I just desired to reconcile and restore our relationship. I realized that at this moment, the steering wheel was in my hand and I was the driver of this vehicle of restoration. Nonetheless, I allowed the Lord to drive. I was on the passenger side. He knew what was best for me. I needed guidance and direction greatly. The ball was in my hand and I didn't want it to slip away. So I trusted God even if He chose to mash the gas, stomp on the brakes, or turn the signal light on the direction that appeared to me as the wrong way.

I was persuaded that he knew what was best. I needed Him! In contrast to my relationship with my ex-wife and other opportunities that I had blown, I was very cautious and careful with this opportunity. Let me say, God didn't go beyond the speed limit as I allowed Him to drive. God is wise at not breaking the law, but He is wise enough to break the law just to bless you. Every rule and regulation that was required was reversed for my good. The Lord made sure that my license and insurance was valid and that my tag was straight. So if for some reason the "police" decided to pull me over, they would see that I (with the assistance of the Lord) was decent and in order.

Do you recall the first chapter, "The Birth of a Predestined Child?" I informed you earlier that I was burned by acid and how it completely damaged my nasal passages leaving me with no outlet to breathe through my nose. As a kid, I use to wrestle with the occasional occurrences of the right side of my nose swelling and filling up with pus in the summertime. Eventually, my nose would grow so tight that it would actually burst and the pus would run everywhere. That was so embarrassing! Almost as if you filled a balloon with water and took a safety pin to pop it. Yes, this is so gruesome, but so true! The Lord answered another prayer that I was persistent of for years.

I was on the bus headed to the J.F. Ingram State Technical College, and suddenly my nose began to tighten up and feel like it would feel when I was a child. Antwan and I were sitting on the same seat. As this feeling of agony and seemingly embarrassment grew, I whispered to Antwan, "Oh my God, I hope this isn't going to happen to me now." He said, "What!" I replied, "If I told you, you wouldn't understand it." I explained it to him and he encouraged me not to speak that upon myself. He also said, "Demetrius, something powerful is behind this. There's always pain before power. Just trust the Lord in this and He'll get the glory out of it." I consented, yet, I was still enduring the pain of possessing a tightly swollen nose filled with pus at the edge of bursting at any time.

When we made it back to the prison from the college, the pain vanished. Before lockdown, I was walking across the yard and suddenly my nose began to itch badly as if a bed of ants were on my face. Yes it was that irritating! I used the mid joint of my folded up thumb to press down and rub my nose to ease the itch, and suddenly a miracle was meticulously maneuvered. I noticed that snot began to run down my nose onto my thumb as if it was running water. It was so unbelievable! This couldn't be! What was this happening I thought? I touched my nose again and felt snot. I ran into the dorm to look into the mirror to see what had happened. When I looked in the mirror, I noticed that my nose had a small passage on the side. It was a very small hole that had been supernaturally opened. It was the size of the eye of a needle, but I couldn't afford to complain because it relieved a lot of backed up stuff that was packed inside of my nasal passages from the previous years.

Once again, I found myself leaping like crazy and praising God in the dorm, but this time, I relentlessly shouted, "I have a hole in my nose! I have a hole in my nose! I have a hole in my nose!" The guy's curiosity was on hand, but they knew that the Lord had done something powerful for me because of the last praise experience I had when I received a letter from my biological mother. They said, "Demetrius are you ok?" I answered, "Yes, I have a hole in my nose. Everyone at the prison was familiar with my condition; therefore, they were happy for me and what the Lord had done.

The following Friday, Apostle Montgomery gave me the opportunity to share this powerful testimony at the chapel and many were delivered through it. They were so amazed because they were actually looking at the walking and living power of God in person working in my life. My testimony motivated many young men that were desperate, to be committed faithfully to the Kingdom of God. There devil was still at work. I was terminated from the dorm shortly after that empowering experience for getting off my bed before the count cleared. It was very petty, but it became a catalyst. I knew it was a reason behind this so I took the eviction with a smile.

Antwan and Dr. Moss assisted me in moving my property from E-dorm to A-dorm. A-dorm was a place where the enemy had his throne. There was no light at all in that dark place. After we accomplished the move, Antwan and Dr. Moss asked me sympathetically, "Demetrius are you going to be able to cope in this thick cloud of darkness?" I replied, "I'm a warrior! I can make it anywhere as long as Jesus is riding with me." They smiled and stated, "OK then warrior! Just stay strong and we'll be over here to sit with you as much as possible." I consented and they left.

Not shortly afterwards, Apostle Montgomery arrived to check on me. At the time I was sitting on my bed and he edified me by encouraging me not to worry or feel uncomfortable about being in this atmosphere because this was the Lords' way of sending me to the wilderness to seek Him greater. He also told me, "Demetrius, God wants to use you over here, so let your light shine." I was willing and obedient. Meanwhile, God was bringing the best of character, conduct, charisma and attitude out of me.

On October 21st, 2006, I was injected and impregnated with a Word from the Lord. He impressed and convinced me to go forth in ministry. When I heard this in my spirit, I informed Evangelist Parham, who was over the yard ministry that the Lord wanted me to go forth. We were in the cafeteria at the J.F Ingram State Technical College and I said, "Parham, can I talk to you for a minute?" He said, "Yes!" I told him that it was my time. He anxiously replied, "Do you have a rhema word?" I excitingly stated, "Yes, I do. He gave me a Word." He said, "O.k. Demetrius, I'll arrange for you to minister on Sunday, October 29th, 2006." I agreed and appreciated him for allowing me to have the opportunity. He was never a hindrance to allowing the Lord to utilize me.

On October 29th, 2006, hundreds of individuals gathered on the yard in G-dorm to hear the Word. People showed up that I never saw before. It was so packed and the Lord moved powerfully. My first message was preached out of the Gospel of St. Mark 2:15-17. The subject of the sermon was titled, "THANK YOU LORD FOR COMING WHERE I WAS". Countless individuals were saved and I was told by Evangelist Parham that this was the first yard ministry that individuals actually cried out sincerely to be saved. When I went back to A-dorm to meditate, the Lord spoke to my spirit saying, "Demetrius, son you done great. Just continue to be willing and obedient. I'll make you able. The best is yet to come. I'll make your very dreams come true."

Antwan, Dr. Moss, Apostle Montgomery, and Evangelist Parham was so astonished at how the Lord used me and continued to encourage me to pursue in the Lord. I remained faithful and consistent. Yes, I fought some giants, but God blocked every blow that was attempted to rise. Shortly after that, I was transferred to G-dorm where I had recently preached. While I was in G-dorm, I met an individual by the name of Mr. Andre Wallace. Mr. Wallace was a native of Birmingham, Alabama and had been in servitude for thirty-three years at that time, but had had genuine love for the Lord. He had a period of 169 years and a life sentence running consecutive.

Mr. Wallace facilitated a Bible Study every Friday night in the law library. I hooked up with him and we launched in the Lord. He would speak prophetically persistently on my life and would encourage me about life. Not long after my move to G-dorm, Antwan was transferred to Louisiana State Prison. I was supposed to go also, but there was an error on my paperwork. I had an opportunity to dialogue with him before he departed. He encouraged me to continue in ministry and in the welding trade. I hated him to leave because I felt like a portion of me was going away. He was such a great friend and a brother.

On December 6th, 2006, Apostle Woodruff approached me at Wednesday night prayer service and told me, "Demetrius, the Lord spoke to my heart telling me to allow you to facilitate the New Converts Class along with Apostle Montgomery." My divine occupation was to go out, catch the fish, and reel them into the net of Christ. I was obedient and I felt great assurance of this. Besides, this was my passion to reach them, teach them and let God bleach them.

I had a great passion for the teenagers in prison, because I was a young man myself in prison and I could sympathize with their confusions about life. I knew how I felt to be confused, lost, and trying to figure out about life. I felt that they knew what was right; they just didn't understand this invisible war in which we are entangled. That's why it was my duty to reach them and expose the enemy hoping that the Word of God would refurbish them. I also had huge compassion for the homosexuals. I desired greatly to see lives miraculously changed. Those were desperate souls crying out internally for salutation. So regardless, of the ostracizing and criticism, I reached into the fire to grab them also.

I knew deeply that they didn't enjoy who they were portraying to the public to be. They just needed someone who truly loved them as Christ loved people. No! I haven't been saved all of my life, so I know how powerful it is to have love, concern, and support shown to you. Someone loved me so much that they looked beyond the criticism and showed me real and tender love. It was so real it was unreal. This love was love that I couldn't understand at all. I truly didn't deserve this love, but it came to the most disastrous places I'd be just to say, "Jesus loves you." That means a lot to someone who is crushed like I was. I needed to know that someone loved me, same with these broken individuals that the Lord was allowing me to be around.

I really saw the hand of the Lord in my life while I was in prison. In the most uncomfortable times of my life, here came Jesus. Don't get me wrong, I refuse to speak of the delighting times and not share the disturbing times. There were many weary, hurting, devastating, mind blowing occasions. I admit there were times while being in prison that life seemed to be stuck and didn't appear real at all. It was as if I was walking around in a paused world, or in space floating. Many times, I would pinch myself just to see if this life was real. After pinching myself and feeling the sting, I said to myself, "Yes, Demetrius, this is real." It felt like living was harder than dying. Nevertheless, once my eyes were fully opened, I clearly saw what the Lord was doing in me, through me and for me. Therefore, I didn't take prison as a place of bondage, but a place of rehabilitation and preparation.

Me personally, I feel that true success is not success if the struggles aren't subjugated. The vitality of the pot of gold was the sack of silver. They say that there is a story behind a glory. That's so true! I'm a living witness that God will give you peace in the midst of a storm, tsunami, or any other thunderous disaster. He kept me through it all. I was supposed to have lost my mind, but He kept me. I was supposed to have had a nervous breakdown, but he kept me. He knows how to keep you in the most turbulent times of your life. I left G-dorm after being in there for about two months and was re-accepted back into E-dorm.

On January 25th, 2007, I was initiated into (W.F.C.M) Warrior For Christ Ministries that Apostle Montgomery had established. This ministry was so awesome and powerful. We began to go on the basketball court and in front of all of the dorms preaching the Gospel. The Lord was continuously sending us laborers that could assist us. There were six dorms in the prison and daily we'd be in front of them preaching. Two men would be assigned to each dorm. It was so dynamic and I truly enjoyed laboring in the vineyard with those brothers.

On February 8th, 2007, I was on my bed which was next to Dr. Moss' bed, dialoguing deeply with him, and suddenly I felt a nudge on my arm. I tuned around to notice a female officer standing behind me. I said, "Yes, ma'am." She recited, "Are you Demetrius Guyton?" I replied, "Yes I am." She continued, "Is this bed 13-B?" I said, "Yes it is." She said, "Pack your stuff. You're on transfer to another prison facility." I said, "Where am I going?" She said, "You're going to Bullock Correctional Facility". My mind automatically went back to the episode when I encountered the departure from my foster parent's house and I was leaving behind some great brothers in the struggle. It was as if I was only taking half of me with me.

I saw my friend Dr. Kita Moss went from a laugh to a frown instantly. He turned around and immediately went into a very sad, teary moment. As the mood of the atmosphere changed, I softly and sadly said, "Moss, are you ok?" He remained silent. I said, "Man, I'm gone." He said, "I know" in a very blurry manner. I hated to see him like that. This was a great kingdom relative as well as an awesome friend. I learned so much from this guy. I hated to depart from such a friendship. Nevertheless, I informed him like I did my biological brother Jamarr that I left behind at my foster parent's house, "Don't worry. If it's meant to be, we'll see each other again. I believed that with my all because the Lord had brought my biological brother back into my life.

Apostle Montgomery and Apostle Woodruff and all the other brothers were asleep, so I had to wait until the next morning before I departed to inform then that I was gone. Everyone in the prison knew that this was a miracle because the administration had posted signs around the entire prison saying, "No lateral transfers until June". I wasn't supposed to go anywhere, but spiritually I was gone in the name of Jesus. Everybody in the prison was shocked to hear my name called for transfer. Nobody could go anywhere until June… but God! I had been approved for work release and I thought that out of all places I'd be going would be to a work center, but those plans were deviated. I was on my way to a level (5) five maximum security prison.

The officer of the dorm did the inventory of my belongings. In the meantime, I was contemplating on what was transpiring. People repeatedly asked me, "Demetrius, where are you going?" I'd reply, "To Bullock Correctional Facility." They would comment, "There's not supposed to be any lateral transfer, but look I see you're gone". I said, sincerely, "Don't look at me. Look at Jesus! It's his doing! I'm shocked also!"

Apostle Montgomery, Dr. Moss, and I went to breakfast later that morning. We let our true feelings out with tears of gladness. We were elated of the transition, but emotionally scarred because our friendship was physically split up. We were joyous about all the times that we shared together. A lot of laughter went forth and at the same time, tears of joy streamed relentlessly. I had precious times among those brothers. Through the good and the bad we learned from each other. I can truly say that those were some awesome individuals that God had inserted into my life for that season.

We came back from breakfast into the dorm and Dr. Moss prayed God's blessings over my life and that our friendship would remain fruitful and faithful. I was the youngest minister of the group and God was teaching me through all of my struggles. After Moss' prayer, we embraced each other with a huge hug of genuineness and consented to continue correspondence.

As for my spiritual father, Apostle Montgomery, he awaited me in the area of the dorm. I approached him and he was in deep prayer with his Bible opened and saw that he had the scripture Philippians 1:6 underlined. He was able to tell my presence alongside of him because while he was praying, he suddenly stopped praying and began to commune with me with his eyes still closed saying, "Demetrius, my son in the faith. I love you so much. You've been one of a kind to me and a very authentic friend. I'm so grateful that we were able to link together in spirit and in friendship. I never met an individual as blessed as you. You're a very blessed man. I can truly say that you are THE CHOSEN ONE and you've had an awesome TOUCH FROM ABOVE. If people can't see Jesus inside of you, then they don't want to see Him at all. He's inside of you and His grace is so sufficient in your life. The "thing" that He has begun in your life, He will perform it until that day."

Similar to Dr. Moss, Apostle Montgomery prayed over my life and embraced me with love while tears streamed down his eyes. We drove down memory lane and laughed about the great times we had in our friendship as well as in the Lord. We appreciated the Lord for using us on the Staton Correctional Facility prison grounds together to attack the enemy's kingdom. Finally, the officer stated, "Demetrius, they're waiting on you. It's time to go." The Body of Christ prayed over me collectively and encouraged me to stay strong.

Apostle Montgomery asked the officer for a few more minutes with me and she consented. He went into his hobby craft shop and gave me a snake skinned belt that he had made for me. Many guys desired to have that belt, but he gave it to me. He also gave me a burgundy and gold leather belt that had the letters "W.F.C.M." and my name Minister D. Guyton engraved on it. Then he hugged me once more and said, "Son, I love you. Continue to travel with willingness and obedience to share God's goodness on your testimonial journey. The journey you're on is for God's glory. It's bigger than you could ever imagine. The Lord desires to use the light that He has placed in you in that dark place. So be strong keep your head up and let Jesus be Jesus. He got you."

I agreed and baby stepped out of the door with a friend sick heaviness upon me as I approached the main office. There was a major delay on my appointed time to vacate. Therefore, I had to remain in a solitary confined area until further notice. Early before daybreak after they counted the inmates and opened the yard, they yelled, "Demetrius Guyton! Let's go! It's your time!" I got up and was escorted to a dog shed and I waited there until the transporting van arrived.

It was still a good while before I was going to depart because of the fulfillment of paper. On the trip down the sidewalk of the prison shackled, everyone I encountered embraced me with love and encouraged me to continue to do the will of God. Finally, I entered the doghouse. While sitting solitary in this shack, I turned off the lights and began to dialogue with God. I was convinced that my life was in His hands and that He didn't bring me this far just to leave me. I found myself being like Abraham. I was very unlearned of the trip, but I was also very willing and obedient to go.

As I was in meditation, I heard a knock on the door of the doghouse and a voice screamed, "Son, are you in there?" I said "Yes." The voice replied, "Are you ok?" I said "Yes I am." The voice hollered, "I love you! I'm on my way to attack the enemy." I replied, "OK. Be good." The voice responded, "You're with me and the people see you with me also. You're gone, but you're not gone." Then, the voice stated once more, "I love you son! I'll see you later." I responded, "I love you too!" Then he left.

Afterwards about thirty minutes later, the door to the dog shack was unlocked and I was escorted to the transitional van. As I was walking to the van shackled, I notice Apostle Bokassa Montgomery on the grounds "Blowing the Trumpet!" He also noticed me being escorted to the van and paused his preaching just to shout, "I love you Son. I'll see you soon!" I replied to the top of my lungs, "I love you too! Take Care!" Finally, I boarded the van and was on my way to the Bullock Correctional Facility.

Chapter 13
Having Liberty In Captivity

Yes, I must be truthful, the transition had me very perplexed, but I was confident that I was body guarded by the blood of Jesus. On the way there, I was impressed in my spirit that many lives and souls were going to be saved through my testimonial truth. Mentally, I was left void, but I was knowledgeable that I was on a tedious, but testimonial journey. I knew that God was enhancing the power of my connections, but how He was going to do it was my main curiosity.

After about an hour or so, we arrived to this maximum security prison that was surrounded with barbed wire from the root to the very top of the building. This place was so wired with electrical wire that even livestock would actually think to themselves "What is this?" I took a deep stare at this place and said "Lord, where in the world do you have me?

I was escorted into the facility wrapped in shackles where I went through the penitentiary protocol once again. I was assigned to reside at bed F-2 14-B. My bed was at the farthest end of the dorm next to the back door and the window. Whoa! What a place to assign a convict; at the window and the door! Somebody must have informed them that the good guy was on his way because this place of residence for someone else would've been a great temptation, especially for someone that had a truckload of time to serve.

I've seen it done numerous of times. I've also saw the crucial consequences as well. Men would take it upon themselves to attempt to escape, but they wouldn't make it far at all without getting shot or beaten by the officers and thrown into the solitary confinement. Let me tell you friend, prison is very real. It's not where an individual needs to be. They treat you like you're nothing and you can't do anything about it. Nonetheless, it's all on you how you embrace your dark experiences. They can be a stepping stone for greater or higher accomplishments in your life or a stumbling block that's a crushing blow of defeat.

Even though I was in prison, I chose to make it a stepping stone, because I believed abundantly that life was a lot greater than where I was. I also knew that I was not what my criminal records said about me. You have to know for yourself that you're bigger than where you are and make the proper adjustments.

As I entered the dorm, curiosity grew from others. They wanted to know what prison I had come from, where I was from, and how long I had been in servitude. It was a navigator to point each curious individual to Christ. After answering their questions, I was able to get settled and relax in the Lord.

Later that day, the Holy Spirit whispered to me, "Three days from your arrival, I want you to go on the weight pile to preach and testify about God's goodness." He convinced me and I agreed. The first three days, I was in constant prayer and I remained secluded in the shadow of the Almighty. On the third day, I was obedient and went forth. When they opened the prison yard, I sprinted to the weight pile to notice a lot of men there exercising.

It was very, very cold outside that morning. My face, ears, and hands were frozen, but God used me mightily. Before I accomplished my mission of issuing the Word, several men began to reach out for salvation saying, "Preacher, I'm ready come on let's pray." The others would actually stop working out and become very attentive and receptive to the Word. Periodically, I'd pause my preaching to make the statement, "I won't be here too much longer. I'll get out of your way in a minute." They'd reply, "No! Preacher, take your time keep on preaching. We need to hear it."

I was so awestruck at this. What He had spoken to me was coming to pass. The glory of the Lord turned that prison upside down. The place was so dry that I felt like Ezekiel when he preached to the dry bones. God brought life back into that place. Many souls were being saved.

Afterwards, I vacated the premises of the weight pile and journeyed to my bed rejoicing on how the Lord had actually used Demetrius "G-THANG" Guyton, to reach the sinners. The same day, I was lying on my bed resting and they brought an individual in that was a native of Hamilton, Alabama, where I was once in the county jail. I was led to witness to him and he gave his life to Jesus, but the profound thing about this that the Lord had shown me how blessed I really was through this individual's situation.

When I was dialoguing with this individual, he informed me that he was in prison for one count of assault second degree and had been given twenty years by the same judge who had sentenced me. He had one count of assault second degree and received twenty years. I had four counts of assault second degree and other cases that were discarded. Yet, I only received ten years with good time. When he told me this, I interrupted his conversation with a radical praise, because I knew that the Lord had intervened in my life and turned what was bitter sweet.

Days later, I was approached by an individual that was on the weight pile when I ministered the morning the Holy Spirit had assigned me. He informed me that he hadn't seen such boldness before and encouraged me to stay strong in the Lord. The following day, I went on the yard in the midst of 1500 inmates to blow the trumpet. People were very attentive like never before.

There was a great hunger and thirst in that place for the Word almost as if it was unheard of. I imagine that the Lord used me facial appearance along with the boldness that he had imparted inside of me to gravitate people to Himself. The men were very curious of my facial appearance and my boldness. They asked me, "Preacher, how can you stand in the midst of hundreds with an appearance such as yours and have the joy you possess?" I simply responded, "Brother, it's none of me, but Christ within me."

When they found out that I was twenty-two years old at the time, they were astonished because God blessed me with such character and mannerism that it actually camouflaged my true age to a much older and mature individual. People would often say, "Boy, you're not twenty two. You sure don't act like it at all in comparison to these other young guys that are acting their shoe size."

The following morning, I was getting ready to go on the yard to minister and surprisingly, I was approached by an individual by the name of Mr. Melvin Smith, who was the inmate pastor. Mr. Smith was a native of Hurtsboro, Alabama and had been in servitude at Bullock Correctional Facility for seven years at the time. This brother was very strong in the Lord. He applauded me of my effort for the Lord and asked me to join them in the yard ministry. I consented and we together agreed to minister the Gospel on the yard.

On that exact day, I met the assistant inmate pastor, Mr. James Bradenburg, who was from Georgia. He was also in servitude at Bullock Correctional Facility for seven years. The yard ministry was divided into sections. There were three sections on the prison yard so that the Word was going forth in all areas of the grounds.

I was introduced to two individuals named Minister Lloyd M. Austin, who was over section one along with Minister Willie Jackson. Mr. Austin was a native of Mobile, Alabama and had been in servitude for three years at the time I met him. Mr. Jackson was a native of Birmingham, Alabama and had been in servitude for two years at the time I met him. They embraced me and took me in with gladness. We together began to attack the enemy's turf greatly.

Those two brothers possessed a very powerful testimony that ushered them into the presence of the Lord. Each day, we took turns ministering on the yard, and at times, if Mr. Jackson and Mr. Austin wasn't able to make it for whatever reason, I'd minister for the section. We all learned from each other a huge deal. As we would minister, many more guys were being saved, delivered, and set free by the power of God. We had an awesome friendship as well as a terrific time in the Lord.

Unknowingly, God had given me the power to lay hands on the sick for healing. An individual by the name of Mr. Fred Cook, who was a native of Boligee, Alabama, which was where I once lived with my grandmother, approached me complaining about his foot being infected badly. Mr. Cook walked around with no shoe on his right foot for a while due to the infection, but when he approached me, I asked him, "Do you believe that God is able to do this for you." He said, "Yes I do." I believed greatly, but I didn't know that I had the gift of healing inside of me. The Lord used me to lay hands on his foot. I prayed and thanked the Lord for what I knew He was able to perform.

Glory to God! The next day, I saw Mr. Cook walking down the hallway with a pair of working boots on his feet. I smiled simply because I knew that the Lord had healed his foot. Still, I asked him, "Mr. Cook, how's that foot?" He responded humorously, "Preacher, my foot is of the chain. He did it! The infection is gone. I've played ball on it and my foot is better now than it ever been."

I enrolled in theological seminary school in Montgomery, Alabama through the leadership of the head chaplain of the Alabama Department of Corrections, Mr. Steve Walker. My enhancement of the Word accelerated. I had a lot of time to study and establish a solid relationship with the Lord. I took great advantage of the idle time I had. Can I pause to tell you that The Chosen One, A Touch From Above" was written in prison? My hunger and thirst I had for the Word was irresistible. It was as if the more learned the Word, the more I wanted to learn. I couldn't get enough. I was like (Job 23:12), it was more of a necessity than my physical food.

The desperation of a desire to change in my life was to the maximum. I refused to be the same individual I was when I came to prison. I wanted to be changed from head to toe. I desired a real change, not a change of name or a change of physical appearance. All of that was good, but I needed a change of heart. The change that I desired was for the promise that is and is to come. (II Timothy 4:8)

On March 31st, 2007, a lady named Mrs. Laurie Clemons, who was the Executive Director of Extended Family, came to give us a speech pertaining to the vision that the Lord had given her. Her struggle became a success for many. Mrs. Clemons' husband had been incarcerated in the Alabama Department of Correction and she used his incarceration as an instrument to reach out and touch others. She had a great desire to teach individuals how to stay strong and continue to love their incarcerated loved ones.

Her oration was so deep that it touched me in such a dynamic way. I was on the front pew as she poured out her all to encourage us that our loved ones were wounded just as the incarcerated individual was. I had an opportunity to dialogue with her personally. I shared with her a portion of my near death experience and she was willing to assist me in the search of my mother. The Lord had sent her in my life for that purpose. Later on, I received information from her secretary of my mother's whereabouts that was very beneficial to me.

On April 7th, 2007, I encountered an enormously edifying and empowering move of God. An awesome prison ministry from Pensacola, Florida, "Cleaning Stream Ministries" came and held a riveting but timely retreat. This retreat was held all day long form 9:30 a.m. – 8:30 p.m. The Lord revealed some areas in my life that I didn't know I possessed. It was so incredible. We rebuked, renounced, and broke chains of strongholds all day long in the name of Jesus.

I had an opportunity to share my testimony with the Executive Director of this ministry. Amazingly, he encountered a similar experience as I did pertaining to my mother. He went through life without his mother also. His mother tried to sell him as a child for tangible things. That was so astonishing to me because I felt that no one else could be parallel to my pain. As we dialogued, he gave me some profound information that gave me the proclivity of protecting my emotions when it came to my biological mother's decision. He also explained to me how his life seemingly seesawed because he loaned to have his biological mother in his life.

His testimony really blessed me (Revelations 12:11) and gave me wisdom to knew how to embrace my mother's weakness. Therefore, from that day forward, I walked out life in the best way ever when it came to receiving my mother's love. God gave me strength, and great wisdom to really accept what he had told me. I was able to accept whatever would come my way. "Yes" was pleasing to me and "No" was more pleasant to me. The word "No" made me strive harder at my dream. I was always the type of individual that took "No" and gained strength from it.

Days later after the retreat, God had given me favor to be able to go to work out in society. I was inserted on squad eleven under the supervision of an individual by the name of Mr. Darnie Williams, who was a native of Union Springs, Alabama, where Bullock Correctional Facility resided. It was a challenge for a guy like me who was in servitude to learn how to be productive and become a new man. God was preparing me for a new birth.

Every morning before I'd leave to go to work, the officers would give me a brown paper bag with a cheese sandwich, peanut butter sandwich, and a tuna sandwich on the inside of it. That was supposed to be my lunch for a day's work. It was very frustrating to me truthfully, but not on time did I complain. I learned to appreciate every moment of being able to be spiritually free even though I was physically bound.

The first day I was out working in society, I said to myself, "Wow! I was actually in bondage, but still able to clock in and out on an occupation. Even though I wasn't getting paid for the work, it didn't matter to me. I was glad to be able to be in society. My assigned job was very, very challenging. We were working in scorching heat. Yes! This heat was unbearable! Sometimes we worked in very swampy areas. Mostly we were picking up paper, weed-eating, or cutting grass in the 90+-degree weather. It was so hot outside and it wasn't fully summertime yet. I'm talking about the middle of spring in April and May. Through it all, I must say, I was one grateful individual to be able to have this opportunity.

When we would ride around the Union Springs area and finally find work, I'd be the first to jump out of the van very enthusiastically to attempt to accomplish our mission. The Lord had taught me a great deal of being authoritative in appreciating every day and opportunity. Mr. Williams would repeatedly say, "Preacher, you're a great worker!" I'd inform him on how I was in a place where I was learning how to appreciate everything instead of complaining. The Lord had given me awesome favor with this guy. Our friendship had gotten so powerful. The other employees had great interest and invested in me greatly. People in society would see me working and actually stop their vehicles in concern to assist me of any necessities.

On one occasion, I was assigned to work in a severely swampy area that was directly across the street from the Union Springs's A.G. grocery store. My job was to weed-eat a ditch that was maybe fifteen feet wide and about two football fields long. I know that this is immeasurable to the mind, but this is true! Imagine being in the middle of a swampy, deserted, and a desolate area weed-eating! Well, graciously I didn't fall out!

When I accomplished my assigned area, I began to approach the van to take off my muddy boots. Surprisingly, this beautiful lady stated, "Do you need some more boots and socks because you look a mess?" I was not aware that this lady had me under her surveillance the whole while from her front porch. In short, I accepted her support. I received the pair of socks, but not the boots because I had an extra pair of boots on the van.

I sat on her front porch waiting on this lady to bring me a pair of socks and seconds later she came out of the door with a brand new pair. What a blessing! That meant so much to me especially by me being in the temporary position I was in. This may sound insignificant to you, but it meant the world to me because I looked beyond the socks and saw her heart.

While we were dialoging, she introduced herself to me as Mrs. Charlene Johnson, she said, "Demetrius, I'm trying to see how in the world you were weed eating that large field in 97 degree weather". I told her, "I have no other choice, I'm in prison! This is a bridge to my freedom." I repeatedly appreciated her for assistance. She said, "Baby, a pair of socks! You needed them. Your other pair was destroyed!" I explained to her that the small things that others would take for granted, I learned to take great advantage and appreciate it. When you've been suspended from society, then reality really sits in.

There's an old but profound statement, "You don't know what you really have until it's gone." That's so true! When we would go on our lunch breaks, I'd leap for joy, because I knew that I had just left behind 1500 plus inmates who would love to have been in my shoes. They were living out of a metal box. I was able to eat store bought oven cooked meals, drink sodas, or chilled ice tea as oppose to the prison food. The prison food was very gross. I'm not going to try to describe that at all. I will say truthfully that the boxes the food would be packaged in actually said, "Caution, this food is not fit for human consumption." Nonetheless, it was still being given out in the cafeteria.

In spite of working like a slave, I still had so much to be grateful for. While I was on this road, the Lord's favor was securely in my life. It was incomprehensible the reason why God was blessing me! I also learned that the greater the blessings, the greater the enemies I would encounter. Moreover, I saw the devil stirring up a wasps nest in my currency flow of blessings. The boots that was given to me by the officer at the prison were beginning to tear apart while I was working. We couldn't take anything out or bring anything in, but I continuously complained to the correctional officer about my boots but he refused to get me another pair.

After numerous occasions of pleading my petition of needing a pair of boots, Mr. Williams saw the need of giving me another pair that was actually his personal pair. When I got off work this particular day, I checked back into the prison and got into trouble for bringing in another pair of boots that wasn't given to me by the prison. Nevertheless, I'd repeatedly explain my need of more boots, but each time I got denied.

After the third day of continuous threats, I was finally issued the disciplinary action that began to blossom into a big issue because my custody and transfer was in the hands of an enemy. A few more guys that went through similar scenarios as I did had heard about it and agreed to insert their hands in the blender of adversities to make my dilemma right in the eyes of the warden. Multiple of guys would spring to my rescue. They would encourage me by telling me not to worry just continue to pray and stay strong.

This battle was too huge for me; therefore, I leaned on the Lord like a light post. I was very assured that He was able to reverse the adverse. Therefore, I went to all the believers informing them to be in persistent prayer believing that the Lord was going to turn this around for the good. After praying individually as well as collectively, I was persuaded that it was done.

The next day, I was in the chapel viewing a videotape. As I was viewing the tape, suddenly, I got a call to see the officer that had threatened me of the disciplinary action. I was very stunned at what was taking place. I took my studying material back to my box in the dorm that I slept in and accelerated into immediate prayer.

Most times when God blesses you, it worries you before it brings joy because your mind questions, "What's going on now?" Have you ever been there before? As I communed with God, I said to him, "Whatever this is good or bad, let your will be done. I appreciate whatever it is, just be God!" I heard a response in my heart whispering, "Fear not, it's already done! Praise me on the way there." I did so as the Voice requested. When I arrived at the back gate, the officer shared with me that the warden and the other officers consented on allowing me to go back to work for the city of Union Springs, Alabama.

God went where I couldn't go (Proverbs 21:1). That showed me what God has for you, it is for you. Don't let the enemy discourage you! I'm nobody special, just someone that God winked at. I'd like to inform you that prayer possess power. The problem is that we lack in prayer to the lover of our soul. He's very concerned about us, even in seemingly insignificant things; God counts them huge in His eyes. He cares for His children dearly.

The Gospel of St. John 15:7 tells me that "ANYTHING I ASK IN HIS NAME HE'LL GIVE IT TO YOU". We may think that the Lord is not concerned about the small issues in our lives, but He is. Other brothers joined with me in prayer pertaining to this issue therefore, when the Lord moved on my behalf, I sprinted to the intercessors and shared with them what the Lord had done. They were very inspired when the Lord stepped on top of man's requirements to bless me.

I was so awestricken and what the Lord had done, I couldn't do anything but wave my hand. Have you ever been there? At that moment, I learned that the Lord cares about the little issues in our lives. I went back to work the next day and Mr. Williams was thrilled and stunned to see me being able to come back out on my job after being served a major disciplinary. He said, "Preacher, the Lord is really with you tremendously. You're so blessed!" He was very upset of what had happened to me, but I sent word to him by a co-worker to be relieved, "God got it!"

I was unlearned that he had given the officers of a good worker report on me and that he told me that he wanted me to come back to work. Well, when I stepped outside, Mr. Williams had the biggest smile on his face. I've never seen him that bright before. He stated, "Preacher, Jesus did it for you didn't he, I'm glad that you're back out with me".

This day, we were assigned to weed-eat and cut grass at Oak Hill Cemetery in Union Springs, Alabama. As we were working, the Lord had me to ask Mr. Williams to pray with me. So obediently, I approached him saying, "Mr. Williams, can I pray for you?" He said, "Sure preacher, let's go behind one of these tombstones so the others won't see us!" God blessed that day and our bond grew stronger. I was able to meet his wonderful wife, and she accepted me as I was. She didn't see my temporary attire or where I was, she saw me. That was such a blessing to me. She cooked me food and brought it to me on the job.

pg. 147

Some individuals think that you're a complete outcast when you're buried in bondage, but I'm glad that when society thinks you're buried God says, "I'm only planting you". There's a huge difference between being buried and planted. To "bury" means to deposit in the earth, to hid, or conceal. To "plant" means to set in the ground, to grow, establish, settle, to hide, or arrange with intent to deceive. The reason the devil is so mad at you is that he thought that what you went through was going to bury you, but he didn't know that God was only planting your growth of you good.

Tell Him "Thank you Lord for Planting Me!" When you sprout out of the ground and grow, all hell can look out. Look in the mirror and say, "Problem, you're no comparison to the glory that's set before me." God is only planting you! Don't give up! Don't give in! It's working together for your good! I didn't know that He was using prison to plant me for a greater growth, but I am thankful that God is very, very, very, intelligent. He knows how to "get it out of us".

The time that I was absent from my occupation, I was unlearned to the fact that Mrs. Charlene Johnson was very concerned about me. We'd finally finished our routes and was back on Parker Street which was Mrs. Johnson's area of residence. When we got there, I was assigned to weed-eat once again. No! Not the whole area like before, only around the mailboxes and signs. I glanced on Mrs. Johnson's porch to see her sitting there with a very brilliant and bountiful smile on her countenance. I waved at her and she waved back saying to me, "Son, how are you doing?" I replied, "I can't complain at all!"

Suddenly, Mr. Williams shouted, "Preacher, I forgot to tell you that Mrs. Johnson asked me about you yesterday!" He informed her of what had happened to me and how the Lord had intervened. The Lord gave me great favor through Mrs. Johnson. She cooked me deer meat that will make you want to slap your wife with a cooking utensil and say, "I knew it was something missing!" No, don't do that! I'm just joking! Moreover, I must say Mrs. Johnson could cook. She took care of me greatly. She'd also encourage me to stay strong and continue to do the right thing, get out of prison, and pursue my purpose in life. She said something to me that cleaved to my spirit, "Son, the very first day I met you, I haven't ceased to pray for you yet!" I smiled and went back to the van to depart for another worksite.

As we left I screamed, "Goodbye, Mrs. Johnson!" She waved relentlessly. The favor of the Lord was so enriched in my life that other co-workers would grow to be envious of me. It's a tussle to be blessed. You have to deal with the haters, perpetrators, etc... It's a challenge, but when God blesses you, the world can be on fire, it don't matter at all. Favor will create hate from individuals that you'd never dream of. They could have a Chrysler 300 and you can have some beat up British Knight shoes with the light on them that light up every step you take and yet, if favor is on your life people will hate you. Ask Joseph!

Furthermore, that still didn't stop him from being blessed. As a matter of fact, that's God motivating factor to bless you. The more they hate you watch the blessings pile up. The Lord allowed a challenge to tiptoe upon me one particular day that proved to me that I was really changed on the inside. I was at work and this individual that was very envious of me grew bold and stood up in my face calling me everything but a child of God and threatened to fight me. This was my Christian brother, so this was an unusual challenge to me because laying on the cracks of the crevices of my insides; I was "G-THANG".

I was supposed to grease this guy really good, but something on the inside of me yielded me with a silent shout, "Demetrius, don't do it! It's a test! Don't do it!" So, when I'd usually committed an assault crime, I turned around and walked away with a smile saying, "God bless you my brother." Can I come from my spirituality for a minute and come to earth for a split second? The flesh most definitely arose.

No doubt, "G-THANG" screamed at me, "What's wrong with you? Who does he think he is? I must prove myself to him! He doesn't know me for real!" Therefore, I thank the Lord for the Holy Spirit. That showed me that my desires were disintegrated. It was none of me anymore. I looked down at myself and thought, this cannot be real! I know this just didn't happen! You meant to tell me that I let that slide and said God bless you! The Lord had shown me that I was changed authentically. I know without doubt that God put a star in my crown when I passed that test.

Guess what! The next day, I was blessed tremendously. I was given a job change from squad eleven to Housing Authority. Housing Authority was the best jobs you could get. Everybody that was able to work in society desired to have this job. With no struggle, I was asked to be inserted on the

Housing Authority squad. As bad as I hated to leave Mr. Williams, I took the open position of being an employee at the Housing Authority squad. I could actually smell the hate, jealousy, and envious spirits on the other guys. My nasal passages were collapsed and physically I had no sense of smell, but spiritually I could smell the aroma of hate and envy in the atmosphere of the ones who allowed it to be injected inside of them.

In the month I was on this squad, the Lord's favor was rabbit trailing me. I met some wonderful individuals that were helping hands for me. Some would cook me food and bring it to me. Some would go to the store for me if I requested and some would encourage me to hold on. It was indeed a blessing.

My supervisor was a deacon of the local church in the Union Springs area. Unbelievably, he'd leave me in the house with the "free world" people. I'd have an assigned job to accomplish and he'd go elsewhere to work. There was no supervisor over me at all. I felt so free! I had my tools and my own truck etc... This was true liberty in captivity. People would accept me as I worked in their houses. Most of them would say, "Young man, you're a blessed individual!" I was able to dialogue with these individuals, sit down to eat food that they prepared, watch television, and was a part of whatever else transpired.

My bottom lip fell to the floor in shock. Periodically, my supervisor would stop to check on me to notice me talking to the people. He'd smile and said, "One thing about you Demetrius, you're not intimidated to talk are you? That's good, have fun! You're free when you're with me! I'm not going to treat you like you're at that hell hole. You're a man in society so that is how I'm going to treat you, like a man in society." I smiled, consented, and blessed the Lord for His goodness.

Mr. Williams would occasionally pass by seeing me in the yard of the particular person's apartment that I'd be working at and blow the horn, hollering out the window, "Preacher, I miss you!" I was able to witness to groups of ruffians about Jesus that were hanging on the street corners. They were very receptive. I knew that they were lacking love and with the permission of my supervision, I was able to commune with these bright children.

An individual was caught trying to smuggle drugs into the prison, therefore they ejected him from the squad he was on and inserted me in his position. That was very fluctuating for me because I had fell in love with this work site. The next day after this guy was falsely caressed in his mind by the enemy to attempt to smuggle drugs into the prison, I went in his place on squad five. I adored this job also because all I had to do was weed-eat around the state signs all over the country. This was a job working for the State Highway Department. The blessed thing about it was that I was by myself in a state truck and a supervisor. My supervisor on this particular job was a very good person from Tuskegee, Alabama. I enjoyed his company because he'd always encourage me in a positive way.

We would travel in several counties such as Pike, Barbour, Macon, Lee, Montgomery, and, Bullock counties only weed eating around the road signs and guardrails. I didn't stay there long at all, maybe 3 weeks or so. As I previously stated earlier, the enemy is always on the prowl trying to steal, kill, and destroy. I found a brand new pair of Sean John sunglasses in the leather case on the side of road as I was picking up paper. When I found them, I informed my supervisor that I had them and I wanted to keep them.

I got permission from him to send them home. Therefore, I wrote a note to my family informing them that I had found the sunglasses and I desired for them to keep them for me until I was released. I had to leave the sunglasses in the van because I wasn't able to bring to the prison. So I fixed a box, self-addressed it, and wrapped the sunglasses up in the box neatly until the next day because I had to go back into the prison to accumulate some stamps to be able to send them off.

Well, when I came back out the next day hoping to be able to submit my package to my family, somehow the back gate officer was informed that I was in preparation of forwarding my sunglasses home. As I approached the back gate, I was told to go in the fence where all transfers would be placed. I was enthused because I actually thought that I was on transfer. Nonetheless, I wasn't on transfer. I was on my way to solitary confinement. I was so befuddled at this fact because I was unlearned that it was over the sunglasses that I found on the side of the road in Tuskegee, Alabama.

As I sat in the fence, I wondered deeply what was going on. Minutes later, the captain and sergeant approached the fence with my box in his hand. They both asked me, "Mr. Guyton, what's in this box?" I replied, "A pair of sunglasses that I found on the side of the road in Tuskegee along with a note that stated, "Hey family, I found these sunglasses and I'm submitting them to you all to keep for me until I get out, Thanks a lot. Love Always, Your son, Evangelist Demetrius P. Guyton." The captain screamed, "A pair of sunglasses!" I said, "Yes sir. That's it! Whoever informed you of this gave you the wrong information and the wrong guy."

He was so over whelmed and upset that he was called from his office for something so synthetic. Therefore, it led to an exempted day of work and a lot of red tape once again. I entered the dressing room of prayer and asked my Father to do something. He did! The next day, I was called to the back gate where awaited the captain and the back gate officer. They agreed to allow me to send my sunglasses home like I was going to do. I singed the property list along with the captain's signature and sent my sunglasses home.

The next day, I went to check out and suddenly my supervisor flies off the handle. He was screaming, "I don't want him out with me anymore! He's a problem!" I knew deeply that I wasn't a problem. I had no idea why this guy spontaneously turned on me, but here comes Jesus. I was taken off the squad and was inserted on the County Commission squad, which was a great squad. I was an employee at the courthouse and on the sanitation truck route. For two hours I cleaned up the Bullock County Courthouse and for the rest of the day, I rode on the back of the garbage truck to empty trash that was on the side of the road.

My supervisor and I had a great friendship. He was a person that loved helping others. This individual was also a native of Union Springs, Alabama. I stayed on this squad until I was transferred. On August 7th, 2007, I was transferred to Red Eagle Honor Farm, which resided in Montgomery, Alabama. Like usual everyone gave me there well wishes and thoughtfulness.

When I approached Red Eagle Honor Farm, I noticed that there were no fences and everyone was running rapid. This place was the doormat to freedom. I mean it was like night and day from the maximum and minimum facilities I was once at. It was like a boy's home compared to the other place I had previously left. My first day at Red Eagle Honor Farm, I was pre-warned by individuals who had been at other prisons with me not to preach on the prison yard because they didn't allow it to go on. I thought crazy of this, so I went to the chaplain and asked him was it ok for me to preach on the yard, He said, "I'm sorry, but we don't allow that to go on here". I was like "What!" This is so crazy!" Yet, I was obedient. Let me say, it didn't stop me from witnessing about God's goodness.

On August 14th, 2007, I was called to the shift office by the captain and sergeant. When I arrived there, they asked me, "Mr. Guyton, do you want to be an employee at the Governor of the State of Alabama's Mansion? Governor Bob Riley and First Lady Patsy Riley want to have you as a servant at their mansion. I took the opportunity with gladness and continuously praised the Lord for His goodness.

This was like a dream come true. I was actually able to be working around Governor Riley, his wife, and his staff. It was so awesome! My life was parallel to the story of Joseph in the book of Genesis. I had gone from a problem to a pit, from a pit to prison, and from prison to the palace while still in prison. The Lord had given me great, fascinating favor with the central people of the State of Alabama. I was given a tour through their mansion and the other houses that they owned. They had bought the whole block of South Perry Street in Montgomery, Alabama.

As I walked into the mansion, my heart was very elated. It was unbelievable! I was actually there. I worked very diligent for them and after they noticed my sincerity, they offered me a supervisory position and an office with my own computer, a phone and other miscellaneous. Look at Jesus! I took the offer with joy. I found myself in my office by myself in great tears of joy saying, "God, why are you being this good to me?" This was so over whelming to me. They were actually coming to me, asking me questions, and expecting answers.

I had opportunities to be in positions that others would see on television. The events that would go on in Montgomery, Alabama that the Governor was a part of, the Lord would bless me to be a part of also. I would wash their vehicles, drive them, and fill them up with gas whenever needed. The Lord had given me favor to be able to drive their trucks and cars miles away from their mansion by myself.

They would send me places such as to Lowe's, Wal-Mart, the florist, etc… They would pay me for my work, but I'd have to leave the money in my office. The secretaries and the others would be so nice and generous to me. Periodically, I would have deep conversations with First Lady Patsy Riley and she would give me awesome advice. She'd always tell me

"Demetrius, you are a very, very blessed young man. I love you and whatever you need just ask me, and I'll do it for you."

Gov. Bob Riley would encourage me also by telling me, "Mr. Guyton, you hang in there. The best is yet to come for you." I became their butler serving for their 100th anniversary of the Governor's Mansion. The entire prison had started to call me The Chosen One," because the Lord had given me such favor. After four months of giving them service, I got transferred to Decatur Work Release, which was in Decatur, Alabama, but the Lord allowed me to see them one more time before I was transferred and they told me that I could contact them anytime that I needed to consult or if I needed anything. The next day, I departed to Decatur Work Release.

Just like the Potter in Jeremiah 18:7, I was in the potter's hand and on the potter's wheel. I learned through prison that everything God forms He fills. To "form" means to press, or shape from something that's already existed. God only formed you and me because He knew that He had something to fill us with. If nothing was in the body, we'd be ceramic. God is in the midst of forming and filling you through your struggles. Check this out, He formed the earth and filled it with vegetation. He formed the sea and filled it with fish. He formed the air and filled it with birds. He formed the body of man and filled it with His spirit. He formed the tabernacle and filled it with furniture. He formed the church and filled us with His Holy Spirit.

Whatever God forms He fills. He never forms what He doesn't fill. Whenever you're going through a time in your life when everything around you is turbulent, it's only a prerequisite that declares to you that Heaven has a directive to get you ready for the next move. God is getting us ready for a move in Him that makes the demons in hell become nervous.

The Potter loved us so much that even while we were "a cracked vase," He picked us up. When you've really been through the mud you'd be glad just for the Potter having compassion to "pick you up." Hell tried to hold me down, but Heaven picked me up. Through experience, I must say that when you're on the wheel, everything is spinning and every day is a blur. Sometimes, you can't really see what's going on. In the midst of the spinning, look under the wheel and see whose foot is on the wheel. God's got His foot on the wheel.

You ought to stop now and tell the Lord "Thanks for controlling your spin". The devil desired to spin you straight to eternal damnation. Our times are in the Lord's hand. He's closely monitoring our situations. Nothing has escaped His eye. While you're on the wheel, He has his way of occasionally splashing you with moistures of water to wet "the clay" so we will not become too rigid. If "The Potter" didn't wet "the clay", we'd become too rigid, but the occasional splashes of moisture causes "the clay" to have the elasticity of change.

The Lord will not give you His recipe of revolutionizing your life, because, if so, the recipe will become lord and you'll start trying to rearrange the recipe to best fit you. The Lord has a lot of ways to bless you. I'm so grateful that He touched me when I needed to be touched the most. One touch from Him will make a difference. One touch from Him will hold you together. One touch from Him will bring you out. One touch from the Lord and you can take what you thought you couldn't take.

Through it all, I gave thanks to the Lord for allowing me to suffer and learn obedience. God touched me in such a way that I had been supernaturally convinced that my present sufferings had no comparison to my future glory. The occasional splashes of moisture were splashed right on time. Every time Pastor Kimbrough and Mrs. Adine Kimbrough would come to visit me, it was a splash. Every time I was able to call my grandmother and hear her beautiful voice that was a splash. Every time I received letters and money orders from my loved ones that was a splash.

Just when I "the clay" was about to become rigid and crack, "The Potter" touched me and splashed occasional moistures of blessings to wet "the clay". Therefore, I was able to stand the spinning on the wheel when I actually thought I couldn't. God kept me from breaking! I desired greatly to come out of this furnace of affliction pure as gold.

Once I realized that the Lord had my life in His hand, I recognized that being in the fire wasn't designed to burn me, but to burn the impurities that were a part of my life. I'm so thankful that God knows how to control the thermostat of our fires. Whatever your fire is, I promise that God knows how to control your temperature. He knows exactly what temperature to turn the thermostat on. So instead of my temporary time of servitude being called "prison", I called it "Heaven University". God was the President, Jesus was the Dean, and the Holy Spirit was my professor.

Chapter 14
An "I.G.D." Of The Gospel

My ministry life is certainly parallel to the lifestyle I lived in the gang, but instead of being a "disciple" for the streets, the Lord tremendously transformed me to a "Disciple" for the Kingdom of God. For Jesus, I'm down for whatever! He died for me so that I could live for Him. The book says that while I was yet without strength He died. (Romans 5:6) I was informed many times of this individual by the name of Jesus Christ. I was also told that He loved us so much that He gave Himself to death. Moreover, I thought this was a bunch of made up words.

During the lowest times of my life, He made Himself visible. When the people that I thought were the most important people vanished, He made Himself visible. I found out that He dealt with the shame and affliction just for you and me. He was despised and rejected of men. He was a man of sorrows and joy, acquainted with grief. He bore our grief and carried our sorrows. He was wounded for our transgressions, bruised for our iniquities, and the chastisement of our peace was upon Him.

Therefore, when He was horrifically beaten, we were heroically healed. He was oppressed and afflicted, yet opened not His mouth. He was brought as a lamb to the slaughter. As a sheep before her shearers is dumb, so Jesus opened not His mouth. He was taken from prison and from judgment. He was cut off the land of the living, for the transgression of us. He made His grave with the wicked because He had done no violence. Yet, it pleased the Lord to bruise His only Son for us. (Isaiah 53:3-10)

All I was ever seeking was a genuine man, a role model, "a real gangster" that I could pattern. All of the individuals that I thought were notorious were actually nothing compared to this Man named Jesus. This Man was, is, and always will be an "Original Gangster". I learned that Jesus is a Man of His Word. Others would tell me in my thuggish days, "G-THANG", you don't have to worry about anything. I'm with you. I got you", and would always failed at their words.

Jesus told me, "Son, I'll never leave you, nor forsake you. I'm always with you even until the end of the world. This was my type of Guy ... a Man of His Word. Truthfully, I couldn't contain the consistency of the continuous and unconditional love that this Man had towards me because I had been hurt, scarred, and betrayed by so many all of my life. I thought, "Jesus, I've heard all of that stuff before! They all say that they'll be with me and eventually abandon me."

I refused to allow another individual to get close to me. Suddenly, a beautiful picture was painted in my view that was really a love bait that I bit. In short, it was only a hook that wisely reeled me into a Man that became the love of my life. Yeah! I said it! A Man who became the love of my life! I don't care! You can call me a homosexual all you want, but this Man rocked my world! He got intimate with me by only speaking to me. His voice impregnated me with power, authority, potential, possibility, security, character, high-esteem, great attitude, charisma, integrity, dignity, praise, worship and thanksgiving.

When He got through making love verbal and spiritual to me, I felt brand new. I could smile brightly again. I could trust and invest into fellowship again. Similar to a woman who had been wounded with past relations and finally she found the one who would actually love her just for her. Can you imagine her emotions? She doesn't care what you say about her and you had better not say anything crazy about her "spouse". If you do, "it's on." She will be down for whatever when it comes to her man.

After this Guy was done penetrating me with the Words He spoke, I was knocked off my feet. This is very sensitive to me and I'm intimidated to tell you this, because what I'm going to tell you will freak you out! Please don't think different of Evangelist Demetrius P. Guyton. I'm just telling you what went on "behind closed doors".

As I was lying down in my bed of affliction, suddenly, I heard a Voice say very gently, "Hey Demetrius, can I whisper something sweet in your ear?" I can hear your heart crying out for me. It's saying come on in, come on in, come on in and save me. I straightway turned on the light to notice no one around. My door was locked. My window was closed and locked. I looked under the bed and behind the dressers. I even looked in the closet, but no one was there!

Click! I turned off the light. Seconds passed of me being perplexed because I was trying to figure out who had whispered to me and where it came from, I heard a whisper once more saying, "Can I whisper something sweet into your ear?" I didn't want to make myself look like a fool to the fly that was on the wall in my room, so I remained in the bed.

My conscious yelled, "Who is this saying can I whisper something sweet in your ear?" "Am I going crazy"? I thought to myself. Eventually, the Whisperer whispered again the same words, "Can I whisper something sweet into your ear?" My mouth was sealed as if it was sealed with wood constructor's glue, but my heart screamed, "Yes! Yes! Yes! Tell me what I need to hear! My life is so wrecked and I'm very vulnerable." Surprisingly, my heart and the whisperer had a deep conversation as I was consciously stunned in awe.

The Whisperer said, "First, let me start by telling you I'm not trying to get in your mind. I want to know your insecurities and all of your in betweens." My heart replied, "This sounds good, but I've heard that all of my life." The Whisperer stated, "I know, I was there when all of those synthetic individuals approached you. They caught you vulnerable, just like I have you. "My heart frowned surprisingly while saying, "See, I knew it! You're like everyone else... FULL OF GAMES!

The Whisperer replied, "I'm not like everyone else! He said, "Please, don't compare me to anyone else. My heart's eyebrow arched in astonishment and said, "Why did you become angry because I said you're like everyone else? The Whisperer answered, "My nickname is Jealous, I share with no one!" That's why I approached you in your most wounded time, because I really want you to see that I can treat you so much better than the others that were in your life."

My heart spoke meticulously to the Whisperer, "Jealous! That's your nickname? I don't need to be adjoined to anyone that's jealous, especially if that's your nickname. It's something to have the description, but another thing to possess the name." The Whisperer stated, "My nickname is Jealous, because when your old friends see how I take the foolish thing to confound the wise and the base thing to confound the highest, they'll have to admit that I'm great! I'm able to take you which are now at the base of your life, and make you of my prize possession." He continued to say, "My wisdom at its weakest is wiser than anybody you've chose to be in your life. My weakness is stronger than who you adored. Even when I'm foolish, I'm wiser." Then the Whisperer continued to say, "Heart of Demetrius P. Guyton". My heart said, "Yes". The Whisperer replied, "Let me be candid with you. To keep you from being in a battle to distinguish who I am, let me tell you." My heart relaxed in its chair, let the recliner back, and asked a white blood cell to go to the refrigerator to get him some iced tea.

The white blood cell sprinted to the refrigerator, got my heart some iced tea, went into the dresser's drawer, and located a pair of "Ray-Ban" glasses with a pad and an ink pen. The white blood cell jogged back to the bedroom where my heart was and gave my heart the iced tea that he had asked for. My heart noticed a pair of "Ray Ban" sunglasses, an ink pen, and a notepad in the white blood cell's hand and asked him, "Why did you bring those additional items with you when I only asked you for iced tea?"

White blood cell replied, "Heart, I believe that the Whisperer really have some profound information to issue you that's unprecedented to you. The reason I brought these "Ray-Ban" sunglasses was for your safety and security." My heart said, "What do you mean for my safety and security?" White blood cell replied, "When the Whisperer gets through whispering into your ears, your cloudy days will instantly become "SONNY". Therefore, the glory from the rays of the "SON" will be so bright, beautiful and bountiful; your natural pupils could not contain the capacity."

My heart said, "Well white blood cell, my friend, why do you have an ink pen and a note pad?" White blood cell stated very humorously,

"Because today is your day! I'm going to write this down and frame it, because I know that when this experience is over, YOU WILL NEVER BE THE SAME."

Spontaneously and astonishingly, The Whisperer spoke above His normal volume and said to my heart, "I didn't come to break up a happy home. I am not going to invade what you desire. If you're comfortable and satisfied with where you are now, then so be it, but if you desire to have your brokenness healed, I'm the One to possess." My heart stood with its eyes bucked, but before it could reply, The Whisperer said, "Heart of Demetrius P. Guyton, I can't help but wait on you. I am so in love with you. I must have you to myself.

When life crams you to the wall and it seems like there's no hope, I'll be there in the midst with you. I love you so much that if I have to be the last result I'm here. I want you to see you the way I see you. I have chosen you to myself at the beginning of the world. Before you were formed in your mother's womb, I knew you and was madly in love with you. I wanted you so bad, that I intervened when the adversary intended to destroy your life. I love you so much that I died for you."

He continued to say, "I wasn't supposed to die, you was. When death was tiptoeing upon you, I screamed No! Not Him! I'll do it! Let him live! Please! Let him Live!" My heart was massaged and caressed with those abducting words that the Whisperer shared. My heart fell so emotional at His Words, that he found his hands being very sweaty, my nerves were wrecked, my knees weak, and my thoughts were racing rapidly.

My heart was in a debate with its decisions that it had made previously of not allowing anyone else to be attached to me anymore. My heart nudged white blood cell and said, "White blood cell, I said that I'll never let another individual get close to me anymore but….this Voice is fulfilling my vulnerability in such a vehement way." My heart whispered thinking that The Whisperer couldn't hear what he would say to white blood cell, "I'm falling in love with the Words that this Voice is submitting in my spirit. It doesn't only sound good, but it feels good. As He speaks, I feel a huge release. My shackles are broken and my strong holds are shredded.

It's something about this Man! If His Voice has the power to do this to me, what about His actions?" White blood cell said, "I was dialoging with my first cousin red blood cell the other day and he told me that he was running through the veins of a changed heart and it was so dynamic. The leaks of its broken heart were sealed, the wounds were healed, and the genuineness in that changed heart was revealed. Heart, if you know like I do, you'd better give it a try. If The Whisperer loves you while you're on the floor, what about when you reach the table."

My heart thought very deeply while the Whisperer laid back in His lounge with a sincere smile on His face…..waiting on my heart's decision to say "yes". Finally, my heart said, "Whoever you are, apparently you're a very incomprehensible, immeasurable, immutable, and incorruptible individual. Therefore, I dialogued with my good friend and he said that he was communing with his first cousin. He informed me that when he was running through the veins of a changed heart, something dynamic took place, and yet, the new heart that had the same body was healed, happy and hungry for more."

The Whisperer said, "Heart of Demetrius P. Guyton, when the SON set you free, you're free indeed. I'm your everything. Without me you can do nothing." So my heart concentrated deeply on the Words of the Whisperer and said, "I don't want to prolong this date! When can we get acquainted?" The Whisperer replied, "I'm ready when you are!"

My heart got very mesmerized with the Words of the Whisperer and replied, "Continue to talk to me while I listen". The Whisperer took control of the conversation and sparked a fire in the heart of Demetrius P. Guyton that he never thought was there. He said to my heart, "Everything that you've been searching for is in me. I allowed all of the poor moments to occur in your life for such a time as this. Now, let me pour my heart into your heart, so that the SON can shine much brighter. More so, you also need to get the notepad that white blood cell has and write My Word in the tablet of your heart."

He continued to say, "I've been your "Original Gangster". I'm the "O.G of all O.G.s." I was with you then and am with you now. As a matter of a fact, I'll be with you when the world is on fire. If you ascend to Heaven, I will be there. If you make up your bed in hell, behold I will be there. If you take up the wings and dwell to the uttermost parts of the sea, even there I shall lead you and my right hand shall hold you. Whiter shall you go from my spirit? Where can you flee from my presence? I'm acquainted with you and all of your ways. There's not a word that you can utter that I don't know altogether."

My heart interrupted the Whisperer and said, "Who are you? How do you know all of this about me?" The Voice only continued to say, "I know how many hairs you have on your head. I know your uprising and your down sitting. I also understand your thoughts afar off. That's why I tiptoed on your bedside of affliction and spoke softly in your ears, "Can I whisper something sweet in your ear?" I understand that you thought to throw your life in, but I wanted you to throw it out. I see your substance. Yes, you're imperfect, but I died for you so that my perfect will can be propelled through you. I spoke a Word concerning you. I took it to the grave with me. I broke through the casket and pushed away the dirt that was packed down on the casket just to show you that I am a Man of My Word."

My heart shouted, "Holdup! Hold up! Hold up! You got to be lying to me! This can't be!" The Whisperer replied, "I'm not a Man that I should lie. I change not! I died and got up again for you. My heart said, "How could you have done this for me when I wasn't established until 1984?" The Whisperer replied, "I've chosen you in Me before the foundations of the world. Before you were thought of, I had you in mind." Suddenly, there was a great pause in the conversation. My heart began to weep and tell the Whisperer, "I'm so sorry! I didn't know that you did all of this for me! How can I reimburse you for your all?"

The Whisperer commented, "Heart, all you have to do is believe in My Son and confess with your mouth. My heart said, "That's it! That's all I have to do! That's no problem! The Whisperer said, "In order to do so and live blessed, you're going to need me each and every day of your new life. You need a Man that's able to stay and stand in a time of insecurities and uncertainties. Let me warn you, those old "spouses" will try to approach you because they'll recognize that the Man you have in your life now have changed you from inside out, not outside in.

You were fearfully and wonderfully made. You weren't an accident! You weren't a mistake, mishap, or a fluke of nature. You were made, chosen, sanctified, and ordained for Myself. I'm the "Gangster" that you wanted to meet. You were outstanding and radical on the enemy's' side, now I want you to be twice as radical for Me. My heart said to itself, "I got to tip my hat off to this Man. That's my type of Guy. I've heard and dealt with many notorious people throughout life, but once I heard this "Voice", it was like none other.

Come on back to earth with me will you? This Whisper that my heart was communing with led me to seek refuge. I knew that it was a person bigger than I was and bigger than the so-called gangsters that I ever surrounded myself around. He became my influence. I had to get acquainted with Him more and more. I also desired to take on His personality, character, conduct, attitude, and charisma. I was unlearned of this Man. I began to be fully dedicated to being abreast to this Individual. Furthermore, I was informed that He'd accept me just as I was.

The voice of the Whisperer chose to speak to me and fill me with His Word, an individual who was labeled as a nobody. He completely revolutionized my life. I didn't have on a three piece suit with the hat to match along with the shoes. I didn't have a "fat pocket." I didn't have a suburban with twenty six inch rims. I was at the lowest point of my life. The prodigal son and I got to know each other very well, with the exception that I actually picked up the swine's husk, he didn't! I was broke as a hee-hank! Yet and still, here came a Voice saying, "I'm in love with your gnat-infested self! Give me yourself and watch what I do with you."

He was so "real and gangstafied" that He took a nobody like me and sculpted me into somebody. After my heart's night of intimacy with the Whisperer, I noticed that I was still carrying this old body, but my new heart was brand new. My heart would constantly scream at me, "Demetrius, I'm changed! I'm changed! I'm changed! I don't have those desires I use to have! I don't think the way I use to think! I don't talk the way I use to talk! I don't even want to hang in the places I use to hang!

I began to notice an unbelievable and tremendously transition. Others recognized it also. They'd continuously say, "Demetrius, it's something different about you!" I'd reply seriously, "You recognize it too!" They'd laugh, but I was dead serious! The Whisperer's Word was so powerful that it became flesh, walked into my heart, ejected the old me, inserted a spanking brand new me. People actually thought I was a walking advertisement for an auction. They'd jokingly say, "What's the cost? Starting bid at…." Then that was my opportunity to tell them about this "O.G." named Jesus who "whispered" into my ears so profound that it penetrated into my heart and my heart responded, "What's this?" I didn't know I had a mouth. I'm conversing with someone I can't even see."

My heart had a desire to become more intimate with the Words of the Whisperer, so I'd opened to the "Word of the Whisperer" and the whisperer began to whisper to me so profoundly. The more He whispered to me, the more I wanted Him to whisper. In 1st Corinthians 9:16-22, it whispered to me how to become "as" others to desperately gain them. When I put what was whispered to me in action, the Whisperer was able to whisper to the hearts of other wounded individuals.

The Lord took my craftiness of recruiting "disciples" for the fulfillment of the gang and taught me to utilize it to recruit "Disciples" for the fulfillment of the Kingdom of God. The book says, "He who wins souls is wise." Therefore I had to be wise. So, I used my gang knowledge to blend in with the crowds. Then, at the perfect opportunity, who was in me would come out of me.

Ultimately, I knew that people would run like roaches when you turn on the lights when I'd approach them with a "Holy Bible" in my hand! So I'd be meticulous when attaching myself to the gang members. I was clothed with a compassionate heart to win for the "O.G." I'd purposely abreast myself to them. I'd walk and talk like them. I'd also spent over time with them to allow them to get comfortable with me. Finally, when the door opened, I share with them the love of Jesus and explain to them what He done for us. Yes us! The thugs!

They'd be astonished to recognize that I was a preacher that spent time with the thugs and the lost. I had no complex with who I would be around, because my heart's finger was to point them all to Jesus. When I told the thugs, the Southern Brotherhood, the Arian-nation, the Muslims, and homosexuals that Jesus was for us, they were like, "Preacher, are you serious?" Before long, the Spirit of the Lord had drawn a sea of disciples, bloods, crips, vice lords, Arian-nations, and Southern Brotherhood, Muslims, homosexuals, etc…..who were desperate, determined, and dedicated, to be a "Disciple" for the Original Gangster."

I was given the nickname "The Preacher with a Thousand Friends" because people from all walks of life would follow me as I followed Christ. The Lord had given me an intransigent and intrepid spirit to go places others would be intimidated to go with His Gospel. Back when I was a kid, I dreamed to be a notorious "gangster" that had a name as the vicious guy, but the Lord messed up my plans, ambitions, and goals. There was a different direction for my destiny.

Yes, I must say, my dream was somewhat accurate when it came to being a gangster. I was ordained to be an "I.G.D.", only not for the streets, but for the souls of the Kingdom of God. This "Original Gangster"; Jesus loved us when we were not even considering Him. He died for us and I think that we should live for him. This "O.G." died for us. Tell me, who will die for you? Don't let anyone fool you! When the rubber meets the road, people will flee, but Jesus. Think about that!

As I think back on many occasions, I know I am supposed to be dead as a doorknob. You too! But He loves us so much that He gave Himself for us instead. Take off your superman and or superwoman uniform and humble your hurting hearts to receive what the Whisperer is "whispering" to you. We all have a story of how mercy jumped the hurdle and grace granted life instead of death, right? Therefore, we need to "keep it real" with the Lord as He "keeps it real" with us.

He's always going to be a Man of His Word, what about you? Will you let Jesus Christ our "O.G." be the lover of your soul or continue to make excuses why you will not do what you know you need to do desperately? I did the same thing, constantly made excuses. You're valuable to the Lord. You don't have to prove a point to anybody, but God. If you chose to do this, all the other things will fall in place. Before you close this book let me tell you a secret.

Just like the gang members, our "O.G." Jesus Christ sends all of His "Disciples" on missions as well. Moreover, you must know that the missions "O.G." Jesus Christ sends us on fulfills an abundant purpose that brings glory to Himself. Don't spend 95% of your life working hard to go somewhere that you really don't want to go for real.

Nobody wants to go to hell, but we're surely working hard to get there. Don't let it be you! Christ doesn't advertise that we need to sell drugs, rob, steal, carry guns, have countless women, and carry large sums of cash to be down with Him. He just wants a willing heart. He'll make you able. The missions that "O.G." Jesus Christ sends us on are very bountiful and beautiful. You don't have to look over your shoulder every half a second. You don't have to worry if it will be successful or not. It'll be successful when you go for "O.G." Jesus Christ.

Instead of guns, God issues us a sword. Yes, a sword is our ammunition not a pistol. The ammunition we carry is quick, powerful, and sharper than any two-edged sword. It pierces the dividing asunder of spirit and soul of the joints and marrows also. It's also a discerner of the thoughts and the intents of the heart. That experience my heart had with the Whisperer was revolutionary. The Word whispered to me right on time when I needed it the most. He's whispering to you also. Let "O.G." Jesus Christ reign in your life. He's the "realist".

He's the only man in history that died and got up. It's been over thousands of years ago and He's still "keeping' it real". When the heavens and earth are passed away, He'll still be acknowledged and recognized as the "O.G. of all O.G.s." The best there was, the best there is, and the best there ever will be. Jesus is His name. He holds the name above all names. He possesses the power that passes our understanding. Don't try to figure "it" out, but give "it" to Jesus and let Him handle "it".

Chapter 15
A Long Time Coming

September 18, 2008, I was miraculously released from Decatur Work Release in Decatur, Alabama after traveling through nine different institutions. I was told that there was a possibility that I would be emancipated in February of 2016. Wow! Can you imagine that?

Supernaturally, I was given another opportunity to be in society. Even though it was through house arrest, I was such a grateful man. The Lord conditioned me inside of the prison walls to be a man of integrity and image. Therefore, beyond the release, everything else had become natural.

My pastor, Pastor Theodis Kimbrough was my next kin that was allowed to pick me up from the prison. He allowed me to stay with him and his family again as a family. This time was so much bigger and better. He really became a father figure to me. He recognized the call and the anointing that had been deposited upon my life. I was still unlearned in the depthless of my purpose. I just knew that I had a purpose. Pastor Theodis Kimbrough invested so much time, interest, and loyalty to me. He also assisted me to get readjusted back to society.

Immediately, he put me to work at his church. I was his associate minister. I became very humble and submissive. Whatever my pastor needed me to do.

On May 1, 2009, I had the divine opportunity and amazing privilege of visiting my biological mother in Saint Petersburg, Florida for the first time in my life. My younger cousin, who is my mother's brother daughter, was graduating from the University of South Florida and she had made private arrangements to have me to be a part of the graduation, also secretly setting me up to be able to restore a relationship with mother. It all began with me being Sunday morning worship. I would persistently bless God in advance for giving an opportunity to meet mom unlearned that while I was worshiping he was working! After service, I received an astonishing phone call from my cousin whom I haven't seen in years.

Ring! Ring! Ring! I answered the phone only to hear a shout, "Hello Demetrius! It's been so, so long since I've heard from you. How are things going with you?" I replied, "I'm great. Who is this speaking?" She replied, "This is your cousin. Do you remember me?" I screamed, "Of course I do! How are you?" We bonded like two long lost lovers and after the connection of kinship; it was brought to my attention that my cousin was a future graduate of the University of South Florida to receive her associate degree from psychology and science. She invited me to the graduation…Of course out of excitement, I replied, "Yes! I'll come. When do I need to be there?"

Word traveled to my brother about our cousin's graduation and we were both excited about the trip. I hadn't seen my brother in years, but we'd always stay in touch by phone. While I thought deeply about this, I began to pray, "Lord, this is the opportunity of my life. You know how I feel about my family. I really want to see them so badly. Please, make a way for me." The next day, I received a phone call from my brother informing me that he was ready and willing to travel to Saint Petersburg, Florida to visit the family. I stayed with my brother from Tuesday, which was my twenty fifth birthday, until Friday which was the day I left to travel to Florida. I had the opportunity to knit with my brother. My brother and I grew so close to each other; it amazed him to find out that I was a preacher, because all he had heard about me was negative things pertaining to the thug life I was living. Truthfully, it astonished me to look my brother in the eyes and tell him that Jesus is Lord and Savior. He was amazed to hear that coming from me.

Can you believe that on my birthday my brother had me on top of his two-story home ripping off old felt and attaching a metal roof in ninety plus degree scorching heat? If that's not a crazy way to celebrate a New Year, then what is? Mentally, I could've bit his nose off. However, spiritually, that was God's way of bringing us together. Yes, in the heat…Thankfully, it was not hell…it was only the heat from the sun. Phew! Even though I was as hot and sweaty as a Jasper Alabama slave, it was astonishing moment between the two of us. While we were on the roof, we began to confide about our current lives. I told him that I was an Evangelist and I travel around sharing the Good News of Jesus Christ and what He had done for me. He was so awestruck. There is a God!" my brother uttered. While we were catching up with life from each other, God was restoring us stronger each second we would dialogue. We shared lots of laughter and tears together. From Tuesday to Friday, we became closer and closer and closer.

On this divine Friday morning, before the sun rose, by the grace of God, my brother and I vacated the premises of his Jasper, Alabama residence and were on our way to Saint Petersburg, Florida. I was full of joy and excitement and I concluded that all of the tears, times of loneliness, and emptiness I had endured in my life to this point was all worth it. We had planned to stay three nights with the family before coming back home.

After a nine hour successful trip, we finally arrived at the Saint Petersburg's residence of our mother's side of the family, thanks to the G.P.S. navigational system. (God's Protection Service) My dream had actually come true and my prayers had finally been answered. I was actually walking into the home of my family whom I barely even knew. My heart raced so rapidly. My thoughts were so tremendous and my knees were knocking because I was about to face the unknown.

When I finally entered into the home and after meeting different individuals, I noticed a brown skinned, long hair, medium build woman sitting on the couch with tears leaping from her eyes. I enquired on who the woman was and they told me that she was my mother. My jaw dropped into amazement. This could not be true at all. I ran over to give her the tightest hug and my mother whispered in my ears, "THANK YOU JESUS" repeatedly. This emotional moment lasted seemingly endlessly. Regardless of how others perceived us, this was our moment. The rest of the family understood that this was our moment, so they joined us as we wept and worshipped God. Worship enveloped the home and everyone immediately began to bless God for His goodness. Love and forgiveness was in the atmosphere and it went from a reunion to worship service in the middle of the living room. I consciously began to think how she really felt about how I felt about her, so after the heavenly moment, I looked into my mother's eyes and said to her, "Mother, I love you so much." She replied, "God is so good to me. It's good to see you." Then she laid her head back on my shoulders and began to weep the more. I felt the weight of her tears as they fell from her eyes onto my shoulders.

I sat next to my mother engulfed in happiness and amazement. I was so excited that I began to do all of the chores in the home that my mother would usually do. Everything she attempted to do, I publicity announced that while I was present, I wasn't going to let my mother do anything but relax and enjoy what the Lord was doing on our behalf. At the end of the night, everyone went into their separate room to rest for the next morning, but I went and slept in the same bed as my mother. I held my mother close and embraced her tightly as if trying to make up for all the lost years of our relationship. While holding her, we uttered repeatedly, "God, you are so awesome…Thank you for your love, restoration, and forgiveness. Thank you so much." That was said all night until our eyes had gotten heavy and sleep forced us to go to sleep. There was no time that we spent together that night talking to each other. We spent our first night together blessing God for who he is and what he'd done.

Words could not explain this moment. I was so awestruck that I really didn't even know how to appreciate God in the way he deserved. As good as He had been to me, I thought saying THANK YOU to Him was an insult. It was so breath taking and unreal to me. Here I am laying in a queen-sized with my biological mother, the same woman who tried to kill me. This was no comparison to any good day that I have ever experienced in my life. My mother laid her head on my chest and cried all night.

Early the next morning, I awoke only to notice that my mother had arisen early to cook us breakfast. I had no sense of smell, but when I walked into the kitchen, it looked so delicious. "Good morning mother" were the words I uttered as she replied, "Good morning baby. Your mother is cooking breakfast for you. I hope you like it." "I love it already mom. Thank you for your service. I love you so much." was my response. After eating the wonderful breakfast that was cooked for me, I began to spend time with my mother getting to know her as a woman and as my mother. We opened up to each other and not one time did I ask her why she did this to me. At this moment, it truly didn't even matter. I was in the presence of the awesomeness of God. He had finally done it. A dream come true, I dared not blow this moment for anything. I couldn't afford to. I wanted her to be as relaxed with me as she ever dreamed to be.

We dialogued about things like life with Jesus and living in His glory and goodness by being vessels that He could use to be a blessing to the world. Ministry was our hearts and minds. What can we do with our reunited restoration to assist others was injected in the core of our conversion. My mother had given her life to Christ during her incarceration and had become an awesome woman of God. The anointing of God drenched from her every step she took. It was an amazing thing for me to see with my own eyes the power of God operating in her life for others who crossed her path.

The Saturday spent together was superb. I could not get enough of my mother's presence. I converted for it. I had to have it. Instead of breakfast, lunch, and dinner her presence was everything filling to me. I didn't have to eat physically as long as she was near me, my hunger was well satisfied. I must admit, my stomach did growl at times, but I felt that it could endure years of her absence and finally get to this point, surely I could deal with a temporal growl. Surely I can do that.

To wrap my Saturday, the second day with my mother up, it was so incredible. I can go on and on and on with the marvelous works of Jesus during this time and on this particular day, but I must get to the "sho nuff" good part of the visitation. I apologize for being rude and involving you in my all day Saturday event with my mother, but I promise, once you read how my Sunday was, you'll stop reading and bless God eternally for His goodness…WORSHIP TIME!

Here goes Sunday… We went to church and amazingly people already knew who I was. With my presence, God had gotten an amazing standing ovation. I saw my mother bless God in such a profound way it was literally mind blowing to me. I watch my mother sing praises to God as if it was her last time on earth. Service was so awesome. Words couldn't explain how incredible the moment was. I was lost for words. I had taken so many photos along with my mother and the family it really made me think that I was in the right place... the place where I should've been a long time ago. In contrast of how awesome that was for me, my time was expired and I had to travel back to Jasper, Alabama.

Next day, I was so deeply depressed because I felt like my world was spiraling down to nothing. I felt as if the Lord Himself had neglected me and everything that I ever desired to obtain from Him had been snatched away from me. The entire trip down the highway, I thought to myself and I allowed, "God Why? Why are you doing this to me?" for a long time, I thought God had played me to the core by giving me a three day glimpse of His glory. I wanted to stay right there in His glory of the divine reunion. Even though I was very happy and excited to have seen my mother and family, I was also very unnerved and disturbed that I had to vacate the premises. No one had an answer for what it was that I had to say... I was hoping that this was actually a nightmare that I'd soon awake from. Apparently it wasn't... it was real... so real.

By the grace of God, we finally arrived to Jasper, Alabama to my brother's house. There, Mrs. Deossie Williams, my Godmother, was awaiting me to take me back to Boligee, Alabama. I had to act as if I had the most incredible experience in Florida, in which I did, but when it was time to go, I had gotten so miserable. When my God-mother asked me how was the experience with my mother, I told her that it was absolutely astonishing, but she knew within me that I wasn't fully telling her everything. Yet in still, she understood enough to let me have my moment of grief. Once I had gotten over the days of devastation, I gained the reality of strength to endure the actuality.

I began to share my experience with the world. Any and everyone who would listen to my testimonial truth, I shared it hoping that my experience could be a catalyst for a revolution for someone else. I was so grateful for the opportunity to actually see the woman who brought me into this world but also tried to kill me. At least He did show me that I was actually healed and delivered in the totality of a tremendous trail of low self-esteem, uncertainness, and acceptance., he also showed me through that wonderful experience, I was holding the power of forgiveness in side of me. So, from that moment forward, I knew that I was God's chosen man with a kingdom assignment to tell the world that HE IS... AND HE IS A REWARDER OF THOSE THAT DILLIGENTLY SEEK HIM... He is a God of forgiveness, restoration, another change, etc. Let me tell you, He is whoever and whatever you need and trust Him to be.

Decatur Work Release Facility

Chapter 16
Scared, But You Can't See It

There is a place in my life now where I am absolutely content and grateful to God for being who He is. He has proven Himself to me persistently in many different episodes of my life, particularly the most turbulent times. I've learned in my own personal life that God is always there, but He never reveal His power until it look like it's too late for you. The Potter never let the clay become dry. He always splashes moistures of water upon the clay to keep it from coming too rigid. God never promised to supply our wants but He promised to supply our needs. Even though I had his tremendous privileges and opportunity to visit my mother, I was still missing something.

In short, this something was my rib...

She eventually appeared to me in the most amazing way. It was an absolute Kingdom connection. God inserted her into my life after a wonderful service in which I was the guest speaker and she was the guest angel. LaShandra Daniels was a very beautiful woman who had grasped my interest instantly. I recognized that she had three biological children, two boys and a girl, and two adopted children. The adoption alone attracted me because I discerned that she was a virtuous woman of vision also having goals and aspirations. The two girls that had been adopted was actually her aunt's children who at the time was unable to take care of them, so instead of them being turned over to foster care, this at the time nineteen year old young lady became sacrificial enough to step in and receive them herself.

pg. 176

I'm very sure that she was unlearned in being an adopted parent at this age, yet she was a vessel that God used to save two innocent young girls who had been neglected by their own parents. I admired and adored that so much about her. To me, she was one of a kind. I also was attracted to her strength. This young girl at the time who had become very sacrificial had become a woman before the eyes of God. As I had gotten to know her, I grew more attached to her because she and I were so much compatible. I thought, finally I've met someone who can understand me and be relative to me. Her life has been an awesome testimony and a living walking sermon in the flesh.

LaShandra, at the age of six, witnessed her mother get shot and killed by her own father in their own home. Her father served only six years in prison and was later released back to the same area where this incident occurred. He never tried to reconcile or even win the heart of his own daughter who actually witnessed this. LaShandra was the oldest of three children. She had two younger brothers. She was given into foster just like me. Amazingly, the residences of the foster parents were in the exact same home in which she witnessed her mother killed. She remained there for five years and eventually went to her grandmother. Even though she had been given custody to her grandmother, her mother's mother, she was dumped into a home of twelve individuals, stemming from her grandmother's children and grandchildren just like me.

It was amazing to me that we shared so any life similarities. No one understood LaShandra just like no one understood me. She had a roof over her head, food to eat, and clothes on her back, but something was still missing. There was a question inside of her just like the one I carried for years, "WHO AM I? WHAT I'M DOING HERE? WHAT'S MY PURPOSE?" We both were free from the bondage of foster care, but we also felt purposeless and no one had the Shepard's Eye to look beyond our problem and see our potential. No one had the eye to see our opposition and see an opportunity. So, therefore, we gravitated to what looked good to us and not what was good for us. We had to go through a lot of trial and error to embrace our self-worth of our very existence…Just like myself.

Can you imagine all of the curiosity of the people and the question that they had to ask? Can you imagine how it was trying to be accepted and feel whole or to belong? Can you imagine how it feels to be embedded with low self-esteem for years and years and years? Can you imagine all the poor decisions that were trying to answer your own question? But when God has a plan and a purpose for your life even when you are unlearned and ignorant to the reality of such, He covers us through all of the dark times and work it all together for our good and His glory. Simply because He knows we didn't know any better. But when the SON sets you free, you're free indeed. LaShandra and I didn't only share similarities together, we had a similar spirit. I clung to the fact that this woman and I had a soul survivor spirit. We are more than conquerors. We are overcomers. The SON has set us free and we are free indeed. We're healed enough to talk about what the Lord has done for us.

Nevertheless, I knew with all of my heart that this was my soul mate from the beginning of our coming together. We dated for a while and later got married. Two alabaster boxes that had been broken could bond together with such an anointing that's able to destroy the works of the devil. Our marriage became an icon for others who would look upon and apply to their own personal relationship. We are so free in Jesus that we look for ways we can glorify God through our love, loyalty, and life. Many people have been liberated through what we bring to the table... And that is Kingdom Agape' Love... HOLY MATRIMONY... I know that the devil is horrified because he thought that he had us but thanks be to God we got away. And we are not looking back... Remember Lot's wife?

My life is so fulfilling now. The Lord has given me a wonderful family that is full of life and love. Every time I see them, it gives me something to keep living for. I feel like my own personal experiences can be deposited into the lives of my children and other children abroad. I have learned that what we go through is sometimes not about us at all. It's for someone else. Now I can look back and say that it was all worth it. It's so amazing how the Lord thinks ahead for others and allows us to go through what others behind us will need to make it. Our lives individually and collectively are so awesome now that no devil in hell can stop us. All I can say is God brought us out to bring others out. My scars are yet visible to others but invisible to me and my family.

Chapter 17
Only God Can Take An Angel Away

The saying, "The Lord giveth and the Lord taketh away" is so true. Only a Sovereign God with unlimited power can orchestrate the ins and outs of an individual's life. He knows when to insert an individual into your life and with His sovereignty; He knows when to move that individual.

Unfortunately, as you continue to read, you'll discover that my wife, LaShandra Denise Guyton, who was the mother of our unborn daughter, LaMetrius Denise Guyton was the beautiful rose in the garden of my life that was suddenly snatched away from me.

First, before I proceed, I can hear the silent questions, "How do you know when God has placed an individual into your life?" Simple. When a person is into who you are and not what you can do for them, then that's God smiling on you. That was my situation. God had given me someone who loved me for me. We loved each other so much that only God knew how deep our love was. My wife, Lashandra was that person that God inserted into my life and we were most grateful to God for each other.

In spite of her family's opposition towards her for her decision to marry me, we were happy. I recall many occasions where she would say to me, "I know that God sent you to me. You are all I ever dreamed for in a man." I was so astonished to hear such words. Her discernment of who I really was internally was incredible. Even though I know God has a mate for every soul and a soul for every mate, it was overwhelming to me to embrace such a strong woman with not only a survivor story like mine, but she also had a desire to please God as well. She exemplified traditional Christian values.

Daily, we would exercise our gift of love to the environment everywhere we went. We were together all the time and no one could separate us but God.

If I did something such as take the garbage out to the road, she would watch me from the front porch until I got back as if I was a child that had been abducted and finally been rescued. Her love for me was so divine.

Lashandra didn't make me love her; she made me want to love her. I had already been in ministry for years, therefore, I had to be more than a husband, I had to be her minister. I led her to the Lord and we together began to follow Christ. Her desire for a greater relationship with God was very impressive.

We attended awesome events such as an incredible mother's day service at New Birth Missionary Baptist Church in Lithonia, Georgia, which is under the leadership of Bishop Eddie L. Long. This was a day that I was assigned to share my story of God's power in my life. It was so incredible. Byron Cage, my wife's favorite gospel singer was there singing her favorite song, "I Will Bless The Lord.

After the service, we had the wonderful privilege to meet other Kingdom relatives. My wife was so excited. The Lord had changed her entire social circle. Everyone received her in the Kingdom of God as if we were already in Heaven.

We also had the wonderful and divine priviledge to attend The Ramp in Hamilton, Alabama where Karen Wheaton, who is a dear friend to the Trinity Broadcast Network (T. B. N.) is the overseer. That woman of God laid her hands on us and spoke great blessings over our lives individually and collectively and we received all that God injected into us on that occasion.

My wife had the awesome privilege to meet Dr. Yvonne Capehart at The New Generation Church in Eutaw, Alabama, where Pastor Joe Webb is pastor. Dr. Capehart was a great example of a woman of God to Lashandra. As she hugged my wife, it was like Mary and Elizabeth greeting. Something powerful and supernatural transpired and this was a life changing experience for us.

We also traveled to my hometown Jasper, Alabama to support Dr. Juanita Bynum. Dr. Bynum was my wife's spiritual role model. She loved Juanita Bynum's music and ministry. Lashandra was inspired by Dr. Bynum to begin her ministry, "REDEEMED WOMEN OF GOD". At a worship service, God through Dr. Bynum called us up to the front, laid His hands on us, and spoke blessings over our lives collectively. Lashandra answered the divine calling and launched her ministry. Thanks be to God, she did. A complete act of faith and obedience.

At that moment, our marriage became supernaturally public. We had no idea that after God inaugurated us, we were to be led to the wilderness to be tempted by the devil.

What we did know was that our marriage was under the scrutiny of Satan.

One of the devil's attacks on our divinely ordained love came from my wife's family who successfully plotted to take my wife's children being taken from her. The income for them was taken, and there were numerous threats from her family and so-called friends if she didn't divorce me. They despised the Christ that lived within Lashandra and me. Our Kingdom lives together were a direct threat of the enemy. He was trying to take us out every day, but we were unbreakable. We were so delighted to be together even though we knew people were secretly plotting our demise. We went through the storm and had dirt thrown on our names. Yet, we still walked by faith and not by sight. Whatever didn't kill us only made us stronger. We were still standing even though everyday was a challenge but we refused to wave the white flag, we refused to give in to the enemy or even let him see us sweat.

They couldn't do anything to damage us so they had us arrested together. To everyone's surprise, they still could not take the joy we had. It didn't make us bitter at all. We became better worshippers as we watched God continuously bring us through turbulent times. Our hips never hit the floor. The plan of the enemy was to put so much pressure upon my wife so that she would fall weak to his scheme and decide to leave me, because he knew that we were a dynamic duo for the Kingdom of God that was wrecking his kingdom. But little did he know, my wife was strong in the Spirit and we recognized that he was using people as pawns to come up against us. We were still praying, praising, worshipping and believing God. We were still standing on our two feet, because we were children of God. God was still supplying our needs in the faces of all of our haters, enemies and foes.

Shortly after we endured the seemingly endless warfare and amazing attacks, we found out that we were having a baby girl. Lashandra was five months pregnant and we had no clue. In the midst of all we had to deal with, God had blessed us with a child.

After already having three children of her own and later delivering a deceased child, she thought that she could no longer bear. She had gone to physicians to be evaluated to see if there was a possibility of pregnancy. The only responses she would get were negative that she could no longer have a successful pregnancy.

Nevertheless, we believed God would see her through this pregnancy and our daughter would be safely delivered.

One day while resting at home, Lashandra suddenly began to feel abnormal and began to vomit vehemently. I rushed her to the emergency room. After they examined her, they confirmed that she was indeed five months pregnant and even projected a due date of February 11th. Guess what, this was the exact day we had gotten married. Wow... It was as if Jesus Himself welcomed me into His Kingdom. Words couldn't explain this moment. I didn't know if I should shout "THANK YOU JESUS" or holler, "HALLELUJAH". With an endless smile on my face, I thanked the physician for the great news, checked on my wife's condition, and shared this awesome news with her as she lay in the hospital bed. After we rejoiced for several minutes, I asked my wife to be excused and she consented. She already knew that I needed room to worship God uninterruptedly and if she were not in the hospital bed being monitored at this particular moment, she would've been right with me praising God. I went outside to a place of solitude to praise and worship God until I couldn't do it anymore. No, I didn't forget to attend to my wife; I was just so excited that I found myself being like David, "dancing out of my clothes". As I was returning from worship, I noticed that my wife was standing in the doorway to join me and we began to worship

God all over again. In short, we returned home with so much gratitude in our hearts to God that our very lives became worship. We thought deeply of what to name our daughter and with the aide of the Holy Spirit, we finally decided Lametrius Denise Guyton. The "LA" was taken from Lashandra and the "Metrius" was taken from Demetrius. We also decided to let her keep her mother's middle name and our last name of course. All was set; we were very elated and anxiously awaited the manifestation of our miracle child.

Only two weeks before Thanksgiving Day and as the days approached, Lashandra and I would shop, shop, shop for newborn girls' clothing. We didn't share our miracle with family and associates because of all we had been through with the evil, wicked, negative individuals, we didn't know who to trust. So we protected our daughter by any means necessary.

Thanksgiving Day, WOW! What a day! It was a day in which we truly gave thanks and fellowshipped with family. We were so excited because we were having a baby girl and no one had a clue. We decided to spend most of our time with my grandmother, Mrs. Ruthie Dunlap. I wanted to inform her so badly that she was having a great- granddaughter, which would've been her first great-grandchild, and a great granddaughter would've been exciting news to share with her, but I didn't know if she would be so excited that she would began to spread the word. Therefore, Lashandra and I decided to remain quiet. This was a day that I was so appreciative to God for, because I was in the presence of all three of my most valuable queenly angels, my grandmother, my wife, and my daughter. This day compared to none other. I used to be delighted about my birthday and Christmas, but Thanksgiving became very valuable and special to me.

My wife held me so close to her bosom as we fellowshipped with family. I was so anxious that as I laid on her bosom, I nearly gave way to what I decided to keep a secret, because I could feel our daughter moving by the spontaneous movements of Lametrius. It was so amazing to feel the movement of my daughter stir up in my wife. I would smile and my grandmother would ask me, "Demetrius, what are you so joyous about?" I'd only look into the eyes of Lashandra deeply with an eye contact that asked the question, "Should I?" As hard as it was for me not to share with my grandmother of our miracle, I replied, "Mama, It's just so good to be here and to be a child of God." Once I said that, I looked at my wife again to see how she received my reply to my grandmother's question and she gave me this glorious gaze as if she said, "WELL SAID BABY. WELL SAID." Still remaining upon my wife's bosom, I could feel and hear her heartbeat as love flowed from Lashandra's heart into mine. The presence of the Holy Spirit was so real. After hours of an incredible visitation with the family, Lashandra began to inform me that her chest was bothering her and it was difficult for her to catch her breath due to her lifelong history of asthma. So we cut the visit short, said our goodbyes, and vacated the premises to journey to our own residence.

Around the nine o' clock p.m. hour, we arrived home, fellowshipped with more family and associates that awaited our arrival, ate dinner, and finally went to bed hoping to see another day yet still excited about our miracle. Around the five o' clock a.m. hour, I was awakened by the urgency of having to urinate. As my wife's head was laid upon the left side of my chest, I nudged her to get her attention so that I could get to the restroom and return to bed.

While I was in the restroom, my wife began to gasp greatly and fight vigorously for air and oxygen. I immediately sprinted to connect her to her oxygen machine and screamed for help as loudly as I could. Finally, the rest of the household, which was my wife's family, my in-laws, came to the room and I immediately called 911 Emergency was called. While we waited on the ambulance we tried relentlessly to revive her until assistance arrived. No response from my wife.

In short time, ambulance workers arrived and we together tried to revive her. No response. This was so unreal! I was actually watching my wife die slowly and there was nothing I could do to reverse it. It was the most devastating thing my eyes have ever seen. All I could think about was our marriage, love, dreams, goals, ambitions, aspirations, our wonderful future, and our daughter. Even though I was viewing this, I still believed that God was going to do something miraculous just as He had done so many other times for us. I had great hopes that she would bounce back from this and this would be a testimony to the glory of God that what the enemy meant for bad, God meant for the good. With all of the praying, hoping, believing, I had to embrace the reality that I really didn't want to embrace and that was my wife was dying in my presence. As others continued to attempt to revive her, I held my wife in my arms as her head laid on the same side of my chest as it was before I awoke to use the restroom. I kissed her various times on her forehead and begged her to be strong and not to die on me. With the last few moments of life my wife had and as she fought for more, tears would leap from my eyes and I would say, "Baby, please don't leave me. We have an awesome future. God gave us a daughter. Isn't this all we desired?"

As they were continuing to attempt to revive her while in my arms, I begged God to save her for me. I did not believe that God brought us this far just to take her and my daughter away from me and to leave me here on Earth by myself with no wife or no daughter.

The physicians begged me to let her be rushed to the emergency room. I was so overwhelmed with what was transpiring that since she was dying, I wanted her to die in my arms and not in anyone else's care. We carried her into the back of the ambulance and headed for the emergency room. On our way, I prayed like I never ever prayed before in my life trusting God to turn this situation around.

I was very confident that God heard me. We finally arrived at the hospital, they took her into the room, and I was asked to remain outside of the room. As I was outside hoping she would pull through this, I cried out to God the more. After minutes of consistent C.P.R., the physician came outside of the room only to tell me, "I'm SORRY, SHE DID NOT MAKE IT."

I literally fainted in his presence after he announced this to me. My mind and body went numb. It was so unbelievable. Words could not explain my emotions. I was picked up off the floor by two gentlemen and as the physician continued to try to explain to me her cause of passing away, I stood in awe. I pounded my head upon the physician's chest continuously as tears continued to leap from my eyes. I ran outdoors and screamed to the top of my lungs over and over and over, "GOD WHY DID YOU DO THIS TO ME!"

Besides, this was the same hospital, room, and physician that shared with us that we were going to have a daughter. Only two weeks and a few days later, to arrive at the same place in the same room to hear the same man say, "I'M SORRY, SHE DIDN'T MAKE IT." I begged them to save my child and they told me that they couldn't because when my wife died, she died along with her.

This was beyond my human comprehension. After the news of my wife's passing away began to spread throughout the community, immediately false accusations began to spout from her family, so-called friends and evil, wicked, small minded individuals who actually thought that I murdered my wife who was carrying our five months, three weeks old daughter. These false accusations sprinted around the entire community so swift that it erupted into other counties, and in other states. I had gotten calls from so many individuals saying to me, "Demetrius, I heard that you murdered your wife and your daughter. Is that true?" I didn't want to relive this mentally so I went into solitude.

The following Wednesday, the day before my wife's wake, I had gotten a phone call from a friend informing me that there was a newspaper article printed about my wife's passing away, and it was titled, "NO FOUL PLAY IN LOCAL DEATH." I traveled to the nearest newspaper box and the subscription for that week was published and as I walked towards the box, I noticed my wife's photo on the front page along with the actual article sharing to the readers that the investigation that was done discovered that she passed away from an asthma attack.

Yes, I appreciated God for the confirmation, but I was still grieving because she was not coming back to me. As I read the article, I learned that God used the Chief of Police, the sergeant, one of the ambulance drivers, and the attending physician to clarify and to announce to the community these words, "HE IS NOT GUILTY!"

This was a very dark time for me; my life was spiraling down to the ground. I felt low and humiliated. It was already enough to see my wife lying in the bed deceased, let alone our daughter. I went into isolation for days and attempted suicide several times, but was not successful. I thought that the trauma and hardship of my childhood was terrible but to lose my wife and unborn daughter was the bottom of the pit of hell. I thought that I was going to crack right down the middle. I was angry with God for not letting me die. Even though I wanted to go under the ground with my family, God granted me amazing strength to endure such a loss. Supernaturally, I had peace that really surpassed all of my understanding, while naturally I wanted to die.

As hurt as I was, I gained the strength to attend my wife's viewing. There were so many threats that moved swiftly through the environment that I be informed by the law enforcement to wait until the biological family vacated the premises before I entered the mortuary. When I finally entered the mortuary to view my wife's body, I noticed that her 10 karat beget tungsten ring was removed from her finger. I enquired of this evil act and I was told that her family removed it. Wow! What a pill to swallow. I'm her family. I thought that the surviving spouse did have all of the say so of their deceased partner right. Well, not me. I was overlooked and completely exempt. At the appointed time of my wife's home going celebration, December 3, 2011, I discovered that on the obituaries, I was not included as her husband and her maiden name was the name on the obituary instead of her new name, "Mrs. Lashandra Denise Guyton". The only thing I had to hold on to was the fact that I led her to the Lord and that by faith; I believed that she was in His paradise.

In my presence in the sanctuary, I was called everything but a child of God. I was cursed out when I arose to share reflections on the behalf of my wife and our unborn daughter. Most of her family arose to vacate the sanctuary when stood up to speak. But I did not fold nor was I fearful of their threats and contemptuous behavior. I said what I had to say from my heart and sat down.

With all of the animosity, anger, and evil wickedness that permeated the sanctuary from Satan's pawns and the noisy people that were there only to see what would transpire from this situation or even to see if I would attend, I was there for only one reason. That was to fearlessly tell my wife, Mrs. Lashandra Denise Guyton, "GOODBYE, I LOVE YOU AND MISS YOU SO MUCH, AND I'LL SEE YOU AND OUR DAUGHTER AGAIN".

Indeed, I hold onto our great memories and wonderful moments that we shared together. I love her and my daughter dearly and will always miss them. I recall her telling me, "Demetrius, if I become anyone great, it'll be because of the God that lives within you". I beg to differ; I have became great because of the God that lives within my wife. Her love for me was so symbolic of the love of our Lord and Savior Jesus Christ. She died for me so that I can live for God. All I want to say to Mrs. Lashandra Denise Guyton is, "I THANK YOU FOR LOVING ME UNCONDITIONALLY".

Only God can give you an angel and take one away inside of one... MY WIFE AND OUR DAUGHTER...

My Wife LaShandra Denise 5 months pregnant with Lametrius Denise

REST IN PEACE: LASHANDRA DENISE GUYTON (My Wife) & LAMETRIUS DENISE GUYTON (My Daughter) (Nov. 26th, 2011)
DR. ROBERT HAROLD JACKSON (Mentor and Pastor)
BISHOP THEOTIS OGDEN KIMBROUGH (Mentor and Pastor)

TO GOD BE ALL OF THE GLORY
FOREVER &
EVER &
EVER &
AMEN!

EPILOGUE

It's so incredible to have people to approach me and say, "I appreciate you Mr. Guyton for telling me your story because you allowed me to see me. Thanks for letting me know what I needed to do through my situations. Your story saved my life. I'm so glad that you didn't forfeit and throw in the towel."

It is so overwhelming and astonishing but it lets me know that this is where I am supposed to be in life. I bless God for all that He has done in my life. All things really do work together for our good and all the things I had to endure were for the benefit of helping potentially millions of others that I may or may never meet. Just to know that I took my life and made it a book is an amazing instrument to encourage others that ALL THINGS WORK TOGETHER FOR YOUR GOOD.

Hang in there. Don't give up and don't give in. God has a plan for your life. You must know that you are alive for a reason. Therefore, when you face a near calamity and survive, you have to ask yourself why. To everyone that reads this book, I want you to search endlessly for the route or the reality of your purpose because He has one for you. Think about it… WHY AM I HERE? WHAT IS MY PURPOSE? WHAT CAN I BRING TO THE TABLE FOR THE KINGDOM OF GOD? Your life is very meaningful and you are somebody special in the eyes of God… He paid a priceless price for you… WITH HIS BLOOD… Just so that you can live in the liberty in which Christ has made you free…WALK IN IT!

ABOUT THE AUTHOR

Demetrius Pierre' Guyton is a man that's truly after God's own heart. He has struggled for the significance of saving others and pointing them to the Savior. Demetrius has a very deep passion and love for humanity and specifically focuses on reaching others who have been physically, emotionally, and mental abuse. His Kingdom obligation is to teach people how to overcome the lies and tricks of the enemy and express the genuine self-worth of all mankind. Using his own past filled with physical, emotional, and mental abuse, he travel the world teaching people how to live a victorious life with a renewed mindset and gaining a deeper understanding of their worth to God. His ministry is sure to help individuals who are struggling or have struggled with similar vices. His motto is "Tough Times Don't Last Always, But Tough People Do."

To contact the author:
Send All Emails To: guytonchosen1@hotmail.com

View his story on YouTube at: http://youtu.be/7X9cWGT54Vg or simply search Demetrius P Guyton on YouTube.

Also on follow him on twitter: @mrsldgx2
Facebook: Demetrius P. Guyton